PURE EVIL

Charles Porta

Olympus Story House
www.olympusstoryhouse.com

TABLE OF CONTENTS

To my Mom and Dad (RIP), Ken, Mark, Haley, Aunt Liz, Uncle Roger, Aunt Mary, Uncle Frank, Franz, Joseph, and Little Jimmi, thank you for making all my dreams come true. Pop, I miss you and will see you again. Thanks for everything, and we did it.

PROLOGUE

It was a dark and gloomy night in San Francisco. The fog was beginning to settle off the coast. A cold air blew throughout the night. The air was crisp, and people were coming home from work, ready to settle in for the evening. Tranquility seemed to descend over the city. All was quiet and peaceful, but suddenly, that silence was broken as a loud piercing sound settled over the city by the bay.

Sirens were blazing, and the police began to descend over a residence in the Bayview-Hunters Point district area of San Francisco. A battle plan was being drawn up. The SWAT team and San Francisco Police Department were making preparations to storm a house that was a notorious drug den in the area. The house was one of the last units that remained untouched by gentrification. It had cracks in the walls, and the paint was pealing. The weeds on the lawn were enormous, and a rusted car was languishing in the driveway, one that had probably seen better days.

The SWAT team and San Francisco Police Department surrounded the residence. A detective approached the door and said, "Open up! We have a warrant to search the premises." No one responded. This was repeated again with the same results. A member of the SWAT team approached the door with a battering ram, ready to break it open. From nowhere, bullets started blazing, and the police officers hit the deck followed by the SWAT team as adrenaline coursed throughout their bodies.

Confusion abounded. People were not sure what to do. The commander of the SWAT team ordered his unit to return fire. The police followed suit. They aimed their guns and peppered the residence. Glass was shattering, and bullets bounced off the wooden paneling in the home. The ground was full of bullet casings. One of the bullets hit a gas line in the home, and this was followed by a huge explosion. The SWAT team and several officers were gone in an instant, not prepared for the fate that befell them. The blast enveloped the home while shattering windows of adjacent housing units and unhinging nerves. The whole area was a cloud of desolation and destruction with few survivors. This would later become known as one of the biggest disasters in law enforcement history.

CHAPTER 1

Detective Draven Overstreet was barreling down the highway at seventy-five miles per hour in his police-issued Ford Focus. He had finally gotten a huge lead on a case that he was working on, labeled as one of the biggest and most gruesome ever by the local media. An individual had been killing homeless women using a knife, and local law enforcement did not have any leads as to the killer's identity. The bodies were usually found in small clearings or abandoned buildings on Mission Street with unidentifiable markings on them. Forensics had identified all of the victims' time of death as occurring after 12:00 p.m. and taking place on the first Saturday at the beginning of each month. This had been taking place for the past eleven months. The media had dubbed this animal "The Mission Street Slasher," and the police were hounded daily about their inability to catch the killer. They wanted the police to catch the killer before the body count got worse.

The big break had come earlier in the day. The last victim was examined by the coroner, and she found a small piece of fiber on the body. Forensics took this fiber and began testing it. Blood was found on the fiber, and it was identified as belonging to Crenshaw Betancourt, who resided at The Baker Hotel in San Francisco, Room 316, on Pine Street. The fiber belonged to the carpet that was removed from the building several weeks ago due to safety concerns and health code violations.

Timing was of the essence. It was Saturday night and nearing twelve o'clock, the witching hour. This was when the killer usually struck, and Det. Draven Overstreet knew that someone else's life was in his hands. He needed to get to that hotel before it was too late. Detective Overstreet arrived at The Baker Hotel, and he double- parked. Once again, there was no parking, and to find a space would be nothing short of a miracle. He raced up the stairs with the other police officers hoping it was not too late. They entered the hotel, and the manager opened up the gate startled and visibly concerned.

"Could I help you officers?" he said in broken English.

The police informed the manager that they needed access to Room 316 so they could speak to its occupant, Crenshaw Bettencourt. The manager directed them to his unit and, when approaching it, heard a loud scream.

"Get away from me, you monster!"

They heard a female voice say from inside the unit. The manager stepped back, and an officer approached the door, ready to kick it open. The door flew open, and Crenshaw had his knife out. The woman was naked and had a plastic drop cloth under her body. Markings were on her chest, but none of them could be identified. The knife had blood on it, and Crenshaw was beginning to salivate. His eyes were dilating, and he looked like he was getting some sick pleasure out of this. Detective Overstreet told him to put his knife down and step away from the woman. He refused and charged at her with his knife. Draven discharged his weapon and watched as two slugs hit Crenshaw's face while blood splattered the wall. He could hear the simultaneous sound of the bullet casings and perp slumping to the ground.

A female approached the victim and put a blanket around her. The victim was cold and scared. This was extremely traumatic for the victim, and Detective Overstreet knew it would take years of therapy to overcome. This work was not for everyone, but getting one sex criminal off the street was a great victory in the ongoing war against this unyielding sleaze along with cancer on humankind. While the body was being carted off by the coroner's office, Detective Overstreet muttered under his breath, "Another piece of garbage off the street." After that, he decided to go the local bar for a drink. Draven had just ended a serial killer's rampage and wanted to celebrate.

CHAPTER 2

The weekend was finally here. It used to be called TGIF (Thank God It's Friday), but that changed since Draven started working for the San Francisco Police Department. His days off were Saturday and Sunday. He usually worked late on Friday night due to the higher volume of 911 calls that he assisted uniformed officers with. Domestic violence and gang shootings were the worst on Friday nights. It was time to let the good times roll and burn off some of that negative energy from work. Draven contacted some of his oldest friends and decided to meet them at Clooney's, a neighborhood bar.

Clooney's was the local watering hole. It was located on Valencia Street, and parking did not exist. It had been at the same location for, at least, thirty years. The inside of the bar was well lit, and it had some of the most affordable drinks in town. Draft beers were three dollars on weekends, and the people were always friendly but left each other alone. It had one of the legendary jukeboxes of all time that featured rock and roll, one of Draven's favorite types of music, from the 1950s till today. Sports was constantly on the television set, especially since the Golden State Warriors were on a roll. A dynasty was being born, and it belonged to the Bay Area. It was led by the Baby-faced Assassin, Stephen Curry, and his three-point shooting was truly a sight to behold.

Draven got ready for a guy's night out. He put on one of his favorite rock-and-roll T-shirts (Garbage) along with black jeans and a jacket. The wind would go right through one during wintertime in San Francisco. At least, that is what Draven experienced while growing up in the big city, and he never forgot it.

There was no dressing up for Draven tonight. He hated suits and felt like a cheap politician when putting on a liar's uniform of choice, the suit along with tie. Besides, he had one of the biggest collections of rock t-shirts and was determined to wear them as often as he could.

He took a Lyft to the bar, which was better than taking a bus or driving in city traffic on a Saturday night. He was there in twenty minutes. His friends were already at the bar, and a pitcher of beer had been ordered. There was Charlie (sometimes called Carlo), Kenny, and Rafael. Charlie was a professor of archeology at the University of San Francisco and was curator at the museum. Kenny worked as a nurse for the VA and was extremely passionate about caring for those warriors who served their country with honor. Rafael was an accountant for numerous nonprofits trying to help them stay afloat financially so the disadvantaged could continue to have places to go to for treatment. Carlo was also a huge rockabilly (early form of rock and roll) and flamenco fan who had a heart of gold but a temper that was never underestimated along with taken for granted. He was Draven's closest friend, and they had been through hell with each other. Life had not been easy and, in some cases, downright cruel, but their friendship was able to weather all these storms, and it made their bond stronger.

All four individuals were products of a Catholic school. They all attended Catholic Grammar and High Schools. Each graduated from San Francisco State University (the only time they attended a public school) and went on to get different degrees at the University of San Francisco. They were all extremely Liberal and believed in helping those people whom society discarded like common street trash. But they did not suffer fools lightly and were quick to put those in line who felt the rules did not apply to them. They were marchers for civil rights in the past and believed in a better world but knew it required hard work and hope, sometimes even putting their foot on someone's neck to help them do the right thing.

The talking continued for hours. They kept playing one song after another. Creedence Clearwater Revival, Jimi Hendrix, Chuck Berry, Guns N Roses, Waylon Jennings, and Marilyn Manson were just some of the groups requested on the jukebox.

Charlie lit a cigarette and looked at Draven. He asked, "What happened to Axl Rose when 'Welcome to the Jungle' started playing?"

Draven said, "Axl was seeing a therapist, and he was probably in semiretirement."

Charlie said, "People keep staring at me when I smoke, you'd think I killed someone or voted for Trump."

Draven said, "I know."

The talking and teasing continued for several hours. They talked about going to Catholic school as children.

Kenny said, "They sure taught us how to think critically, practically drilled it in our heads."

Then Draven responded by saying, "But when it comes to the church, they demanded blind obedience and loyalty. They taught everyone to critically analyze a situation so good that it led to Catholics leaving the church.

"Or maybe," Rafael said, "the Catholic church left them."

Ken replied by saying, "The pedophilia scandal did not help them."

Everyone thought the subject matter was becoming extremely heavy and people were there to relax, not get angry or worked up. It was getting late. The fog was rolling in, and the patrons in the bar were getting tired. Some looked like they would fall off the barstool and hurt themselves on the hard wooden ground.

"Last call," said the bartender, and everyone started to leave the building. Draven and his friends were ready to go home.

Their eyes were heavy, and everyone looked extremely tired and exhausted. Everyone selected the Lyft app on their phones and waited for their rides that would take them home. Draven's was the last to come.

CHAPTER 3

Hamburgers and fries were Trish Armstrong's life at the moment. She worked at V's, which was located on the corner of 11th Street and Folsom. V's was a local diner that served some of the best hamburgers along with fish and chips in town. Trish knew this job was not forever and longed for her present situation to change.

She went to San Francisco State University and studied psychology. She was almost ready to graduate from this institution and wanted to pursue a master's degree in counseling psychology specializing in marriage and family therapy from the University of San Francisco. She worked at the restaurant on weekends along with after classes to pay for her rent and other expenses such as textbooks. It was a grind, but she knew it would come to an end and life would be different after graduation.

Trish hustled back and forth at the restaurant. She took the customer's orders and delivered them to their tables. Trish busted tables and took out the garbage. This continued for eight hours until darkness descended onto the restaurant and her shift was over. She smelled of ground beef and grease and was happy that the day was done. She desperately wanted to take a bath and wash the odors of the restaurant off her body.

She was relieved. Her feet were exhausted and achy. She counted her tips ($150) and said goodbye to the owner along with other workers. She made arrangements via telephone for a Lyft driver to take her home to her apartment. Trish normally waited inside; one cannot be too careful with all those crazy people running around. But this time, she decided to wait outside. Last time she took Lyft, the driver could not find the restaurant, and he kept passing it. She was determined not to let this happen again.

The owner of the restaurant watched Trish from its window as she waited for the Lyft driver. He wanted to make sure that she was picked up without a problem. But his stomach had other ideas. He would spend that time making a donation to the porcelain god.

Trish was outside. "Where is that Lyft driver? It is cold, and my feet are killing me. I want to go home and rest them." She checked her phone, and it said arrival time eight minutes. From nowhere, a pipe hit her at the back of the head, and she was knocked unconscious.

"Aaaaaaaaaaaaaaaaaaaaaaaa!" Trish screamed and jumped. "Where am I? What is going on?" She lay naked on a slab, and the room was dimly lit. The room was filled with computers and other electrical equipment. She could see a figure in the background but could not make it out.

"Sleep, sweetie, it will all be over soon." She heard it say in a silent but disturbing tone. A mask was placed around Trish's mouth, and she went off to dreamland, never to awaken again.

The figure turned on a machine. He inserted four tubes in Trish's body, one at the back of each leg and the others at the back of both arms. He hit a button on a computer, and presto, the countdown for the blood transfusion process was on. He sat down on a metal slab that was similar to the one that Trish was currently strapped down to. He placed four tubes on his body. They were put in the same areas as Trish's. The killer put a mask around his mouth and he instantly fell asleep. The mask was connected to a tube that pumped sleeping gas throughout his body. The computer counted down, and once it hit zero, the process started. The tubes began draining the blood from Trish's body. Once this process was completed, the same started to occur in the figure that was sitting next to Trish on the cold metal slab. After this was completed, the blood that was drained from Trish's body was automatically transferred to the figure sitting next to her. The figure awoke several hours after this process was completed and said, "All done, will not have to do this for another week."

CHAPTER 4

Draven awoke from his deep slumber, and it was morning. The sun was shining brightly, and his best friend lay in bed with him. It was Little Jimmi, his dog. Little Jimmi was of a mix of pit bull, Labrador, and terrier. He had beautiful, silky fur that glistened in the sun. It mixed perfectly with the white fur that was located in the area below his stomach, which led him to be labeled a tuxedo dog by the SPCA. He currently was a puppy in dog years and would grow to be a beautiful pooch upon reaching adulthood. Little Jimmi had been adopted by Draven from the SPCA in San Francisco. He was Draven's best friend, and they had been roommates for the past seven months. They did everything together, but Little Jimmi's favorite activity was watching horror movies, especially *The Nightmare on Elm Street* series.

Jimmi began licking voraciously Draven's face. He did this each morning and Draven looked forward to it. It was Little Jimmi's way of expressing his deep undying love for Draven. Draven could tell that Jimmi wanted to play this morning. Draven said, "Not now, Daddy has to go to work and catch bad guys." Draven got out of bed, almost knocking Jimmi off it, and began searching for dog food. He put some in Jimmi's bowl and set it out for him. Jimmi began eating it.

Draven had a moderately sized apartment. He had a great view of the San Francisco coastline from his kitchen window. Every morning, he watched as the fog came and settled onto the city like a blanket. His apartment was located near the Marina District, and he paid two thousand a month, not bad for rent control. His walls were adorned with posters of famous musicians such as Jimmi Hendrix, Garbage, and Siouxsie Sioux from Siouxsie and the Banshees. The colors in his apartment were muted, and it came with a kitchen along with bathroom. On the wall facing his bed was his television set. Next to his television was his stereo and collection of movies along with music. In another room off to the side was his huge library of books. They focused on topics such as murder mysteries, political science, art, music, history, and psychological thrillers. He was a voracious reader, who devoured books and loved to develop his mind.

He turned on the television set and proceeded to eat breakfast. It consisted of frosted flakes. He added bananas and sugar to the cereal. Some cereal tasted like cardboard if nothing was added to it, and he wanted to prevent that from happening. While eating his cereal, he listened to Sal Castenada talk about the local weather and traffic:

Traffic on highway 101 South was heavy, and Bart was expecting delays on the morning commute. Some fog today and expect it to be sunny in the afternoon.

He finished his breakfast and washed the bowl his cereal was in. Draven took a bath and got dressed. He locked the door to his apartment and brought Jimmi over to Maria Vega, his neighbor, who normally watched the dog when Draven was at work.

CHAPTER 5

Detective Overstreet made it to work. City traffic had been a nightmare. He had taken Uber to the police station and nearly became involved in an accident. The Uber driver was speeding and almost hit another car. Detective Overstreet was pretty shaken up and decided to have an herbal tea before starting his day at work. He was ready to go home and pretend like today never happened.

He grabbed the sports page from the *San Francisco Chronicle* newspaper and began pouring over it in the hopes of forgetting about the close call before arriving to work. He started reading about the Golden State Warriors and became completely engrossed in the article. They had just defeated the Portland Trailblazers and advanced to the NBA championship series. He felt himself becoming more relaxed as he read about the team.

The phone rang, and it broke his concentration. It was really loud, and the noise reminded him that Draven needed to adjust the volume of the ringer. "Detective Overstreet, this is Officer Santiago, and we have a body." Detective Overstreet gathered more information about the location of the body along with a description of it. He placed the information in his notebook, and he informed the officer that he would be there in twenty minutes. Both hung up their phones once the conversation was finished.

Draven checked in with Captain Hammer and informed him that he was going to the Bayview/Hunter's Point District to examine a body that was found at this location. Captain Hammer reminded Detective Overstreet to keep him posted about it and proceeded to go to the requisition office located in the basement of the police station. He signed out for one of the squad cars and proceeded to travel to the scene of the crime.

He signed out for a red Ford Prius. It was a new car, and he looked forward to driving it. The Prius had power brakes, and this was a constant challenge for him. The brakes were extremely sensitive, and he had to be careful when applying them. Before heading out, he scanned the stations on the radio and settled on one that was playing "Welcome to the Jungle" by Guns N Roses. This brought back memories. "Welcome to the Jungle" was from *The Appetite for Destruction* album by Guns N Roses. It was the first rock-and-roll album that he had purchased. He bought it at Musicland as a teenager back when cassettes were popular. This was before the Internet and YouTube. He had worn the cassette out after listening to it daily for a year.

CHAPTER 6

Draven finally made it to the Bayview/Hunter's Point District. He parked his car and turned off the radio. Officer Santiago approached the vehicle and started escorting him to the body. Detective Overstreet looked around and noticed that the area had changed drastically. Gone were the vacant lots and houses that had once surrounded the area. In its place stood the newly built foundation of a hospital that was being constructed along with luxury apartments.

Officer Santiago brought him to the body. It was naked and covered entirely in plastic. It was a white female who appeared to be in her mid-twenties. There were no signs of a struggle, and it looked like she was sleeping peacefully. Overstreet noted that she seemed at peace. Before letting forensics take over, he lifted the plastic and noticed that she had two sets of marks on her body. One was located at the back of each leg. Another was found at the back of each arm.

Forensics came and started to take control of the crime scene. Pictures were taken of it as well. Soil samples were placed in a plastic bag. The head of the forensics unit, Asia Francisco, began talking to Officer Santiago to gain more information about the dead body. She was dressed entirely in black with silver rings on her fingers. She was wearing a Garbage T-shirt and black and white Chuck Taylor Converse shoes. Her hair was black with red highlights, and she looked like Abbey from *NCIS*. Draven had a massive crush on her and almost forgot that he was at a crime scene.

CHAPTER 7

Lisa Miranda woke up, and she was excited to start the day. She made her bed and ate breakfast. Lisa took out the clothes that she was going to wear today. She grabbed her new Jimi Hendrix T-shirt and placed it on her bed. Lisa recently purchased this item at Hot Topic and was looking forward to wearing it today. To complete this ensemble, she selected blue jeans and a pair of Converse tennis shoes from her closet. These items were placed on the bed as well. She left her apartment and locked the door. Lisa made arrangements to take an Uber to San Francisco State University and was there in twenty minutes.

Lisa was studying dance at San Francisco State University. She wanted to be a flamenco dancer and dreamed of working at one of the premier dance studios in Spain. Before doing that, she needed to complete her general education courses. After doing this, Lisa would be able to begin working on completing course requirements to obtain a bachelor's degree in dance from San Francisco State University.

After her last class, Lisa took an Uber to Amoeba Records. Lisa worked at Amoeba Records part time and loved the generous discount that came with being employed at this company. She also liked the relaxed dress code and friendly atmosphere at the store. Today, she would be working on making a display for the new music being released tomorrow. It would probably take her several hours to complete this project.

Lisa completed the project and looked at the clock. It was almost ten o'clock and close to closing time. Lisa helped the manager usher the last remaining customers out of the store and closed and locked the door. She put the closed sign out and started cleaning the store. It was eleven o'clock once everything was done. She said goodbye to her supervisor and went outside to wait for a friend who would take Lisa back home to her apartment.

While waiting outside, she received a text from her friend who said that he was almost there. She began walking closer to the curb so Lisa's friend would be able to see her. Lisa received another text, and while attempting to look at the screen on the phone, she felt a huge fist smash across her face. She went down and was out instantly.

She awoke, and the room was dark. She could see tubes and other electrical equipment against the walls. She noticed that several tubes were attached to the back of her arms and legs. Lisa started screaming and felt the sweat pour out of her body. She was petrified and knew nothing good would come from this. From a dark corner off to the side, she heard a voice say, "Relax, and all will be over soon." She heard a slight click like that of a switch and Lisa fell asleep, never to awaken again.

After everything was done, the killer unhooked all the tubing that was connected to him. He did the same for Lisa and checked her pulse. She was dead, and he began making the final preparations to dispose of the body. He took off all her clothes and started wrapping the body in plastic. He placed her clothes in the incinerator and then completed the process of wrapping it in plastic. He put it in the trunk of his car and consulted a map of San Francisco to decide where to drop the body off. He smiled after making his selection.

CHAPTER 8

Detective Overstreet was sitting at his desk and working on completing paperwork. It was a typical Tuesday morning, and the office appeared to be in a flurry of activity. Telephones rang while some of the detectives attempted to complete unfinished case reports. Draven checked his messages when the call came in.

"We have another body," uttered Officer Garcia from the other end of the line.

"I will be right there," replied Detective Overstreet, and he proceeded to leave the police station.

Draven arrived at the crime scene. The traffic was light, and he made it there in thirty minutes. Officer Garcia approached the car and began to escort Draven to the location of the dead body. It was wrapped in plastic and left on the site where a new residence hall for the students at San Francisco State University would be constructed. Draven noticed the careful detail and attention that was paid to the preservation of the body by the killer. The body was of a young Caucasian female in her early twenties, and she appeared naked under the plastic covering. The dead body was visible through it, and Draven went to inspect the corpse for any signs of a possible struggle. He lifted the plastic covering, and there appeared to be four separate puncture marks on the back of each arm along with the leg.

"Do we have a serial killer?" uttered Ventura Austin, who was an investigative reporter for the *San Francisco Chronicle*.

"I cannot say until we have more evidence, but we have not ruled anything out," replied Draven.

A loud noise reverberated throughout the crime scene. Draven turned around and saw that the forensics team was approaching it. Asia Francisco was leading the team, and she directed other members to begin examining the crime scene for possible evidence. They proceeded to take pictures of the dead body from different angles and gather soil samples. The other members of the team started dusting the plastic covering that the body was in for fingerprints. Another attempted to take fingerprints of the deceased, so she could be identified at a later date.

Asia Francisco took out her notebook and started jotting down some notes.

Location: Vacant lot near San Francisco State University, where new residence hall would be constructed. Body has not started decompensation process, which suggests a fresh kill. Body appears to be of a White, Caucasian female in her early twenties, and special care is taken to preserve it in plastic by the killer. Puncture wounds found on the back of both arms and legs.

CHAPTER 9

Asia decided to relax and take a break from her busy job at the forensics lab. She was reading a newspaper article from the *San Francisco Chronicle* about an individual who moved from San Francisco to Arizona to take a job as a graphic designer. Asia started daydreaming about that period in her life. She had just moved to Phoenix after graduating from the University of San Francisco, with a master's degree in criminal science. She wanted to work for the forensics unit at the San Francisco Police Department but was unable to land a job with them. Asia was told that she did not have enough experience. On a cold Tuesday morning, she received a call from the head of the forensics unit for the Phoenix Police Department pertaining to a job offer. She went to the interview and landed it. Eventually, she would move back to San Francisco after landing her dream job with the forensic unit of the San Francisco Police Department.

It was a culture shock for Asia. Asia grew up in San Francisco and loved the vibrant atmosphere of the city. The city was buzzing with activity, and Asia found this mentally stimulating. San Francisco had museums, art galleries, concert halls, restaurants, sporting events, and movie theaters. Asia resided in an extremely racially diverse neighborhood, and the weather was perfect. It was not too cold in winter or too hot in summer. She spoke several languages—Italian, Spanish, and Tagalog—which was a blessing in her chosen field.

Asia was not religious. She was raised Catholic but left it once the pedophilia scandal broke out in the nineties. She was deeply hurt by the way that the Catholic Church handled this scandal and could not take the hypocrisy of that institution anymore. Asia was not conservative and detested *Fox News*. She thought it was filled with propaganda, lies, and hate. Asia was friends with the LGBT community and hated the way religious people demonized these individuals. As a woman, she found it deeply disturbing how conservative Christians were ready to take several of her civil rights away. But Asia was a gun owner and believed in the use of firearms for home protection. She also believed in responsible gun ownership and knew that universal background checks were a necessity too so they did not fall into the wrong hands.

And Phoenix was the total opposite of this. Asia moved into the apartment that she would live in for the next three years. The neighbors were nice, but they had strong religious and conservative undertones. Asia could hear *Fox News* blaring from the rooms of the other tenants at night, which she chose to ignore. Repeated exposure could lead to Asia becoming angry or losing her grip on reality.

The weather was a study in extremes. The winters were freezing cold, and the summers blistering hot. This made wearing her gothic wardrobe difficult if not impossible. But she was determined to land her dream job and eventually leave Phoenix, Arizona. Three years later, Asia saw an opening in the forensics unit for the San Francisco Police Department, and she applied for it. Asia nailed the interview and landed the job of her dreams. She moved from Phoenix to San Francisco and never looked back.

CHAPTER 10

Harold decided to have a smoke before going back to the Bayshore Navigation Center. It had been a long day filled with one appointment after another. He had finally made it back to the Bayshore Navigation Center on Bayshore Blvd. and decided to go to sleep early. Traffic had been a nightmare, and Harold was relieved to be back at the center. Harold was exhausted, and his eyes were growing heavier by the minute. Harold thought that he was going to pass out from exhaustion and not make it to his bed. He fell asleep at nine and was awakened by a car backfiring outside. Harold checked his watch, and it said 12:15 p.m. He went outside and decided to have a cigarette. Harold knew that it was going take a while for his nerves to calm down. Once his nerves calmed down, he would be able to go back to bed.

Harold went to take a short walk. It was a warm October night in San Francisco. He could feel the humidity in the air and the sweat pouring out from his body. Harold knew that going back to sleep was not an option. When walking toward the back of the Bayshore Navigation Center, Harold noticed an incredible amount of garbage littered the streets. He was amazed by this and often wondered, *Where was it coming from?* The garbage seemed to magically appear out of nowhere despite the city's best efforts to keep the streets clean.

"Where was it coming from?"

While walking around the Bayshore Navigation Center, Harold's feet started aching, so he decided to sit down. He looked around his immediate area and could not locate anything that looked remotely comfortable to sit on. He decided to have a seat on the edge of the curb and almost tripped over something. Harold thought it was a dead animal or some discarded debris. He almost screamed and was generally startled by his discovery. He looked closer at the object and noticed that it was a body wrapped completely in plastic. Harold knew enough about crime scenes to not disturb them, so he went into the Bayshore Navigation Center so the staff at this facility could contact the police.

CHAPTER 11

The director of the Bayshore Navigation Center called the police, and they were at the facility in seconds. It was turned into a warzone, and the once-sleepy Navigation Center lay quiet no more. A perimeter was established around the crime scene and various pictures taken of the body at different angles. Soil samples were taken near the body for later examination and the plastic that the dead body lay in dusted for fingerprints. Onlookers were shoed away, and the police began to search for a murder weapon but found nothing.

Draven arrived at the crime scene, and Officer Garcia immediately escorted him to the dead body. While being taken to it, Draven listened as Officer Garcia recounted the tale of its discovery to him. He informed Draven that the dead body had been discovered by a resident at the Bayshore Navigation Center. Officer Garcia told him that it was found while this individual was taking a walk outside the center early this morning. Draven listened as Officer Garcia said, "We have this individual in custody and await your further instructions."

Draven responded, "Thank you for your assistance, Officer Garcia, and I would like to speak to this individual immediately."

Before deciding to do that, Draven went to examine the dead body. While approaching it, he noticed that the deceased was wrapped entirely in plastic. The victim appeared to be a Caucasian female in her twenties. Draven saw that the dead body appeared drained of all its color. It seemed that the killer took special care when wrapping the body because the deceased looked as if she was sleeping peacefully. After lifting the plastic covering and examining the dead body, Draven discovered that it had various puncture wounds. Upon further investigation, Draven discovered that one puncture mark was found on the back of each arm and leg. He said, "Damn, we have another serial killer on our hands."

Draven informed Officer Garcia that he was ready to talk to the individual who discovered the body. Officer Garcia brought this individual to Draven, and he could not have been more than twenty- five years of age. He said that his name was Harold and talked about being a resident of this facility. Harold told Draven that he recently lost his job and needed a place to stay. While residing at the center, Harold said he was working on securing permanent employment and financial stability.

CHAPTER 12

Today was the big day for Draven. Siouxsie and the Banshee tickets were on sale shortly, and he was determined to purchase one. This was one of his favorite bands, and he waited years for them to come to the Bay Area. Draven was determined to see them live for the first time in his life. He had a vast collection of memorabilia from the band, which included T-shirts, DVDs, and CDs. Draven had met the lead singer, Siouxsie Sioux, during an autograph signing at Amoeba Records several years ago. When speaking to this individual, he thanked her for all the joy and happiness that this music gave him throughout the years. Draven specifically mentioned the songs "The Last Beat of My Heart" and "Fireworks." When done reminiscing, Draven logged into the Live Nation website. Within seconds, he secured tickets for the Siouxsie and the Banshee concert later today at nine in the Warfield theater.

The weekend was finally here, and Draven could not be happier. It had been a stressful and tense week at the police station. The recent killings had everyone on edge, and Draven decided that he needed a break from this to prevent burnout. He went to see Dr. Kenneth Garcia, who is one of his oldest and dearest friends. Dr. Garcia started out as a nurse and became one of the leading practitioners for treatment of veterans suffering from posttraumatic stress disorder in the field. He was a giant in the industry and helped numerous veterans on their path toward recovery from the ravages of war. He was also an avid video game fanatic and huge Bay Area sports fan, especially of the Golden State Warriors. Stephen Curry was his sports hero, and he idolized the man.

Dr. Garcia was born and raised in The United States. He went to San Francisco State University with Draven, and they had marched for LGBT rights when attending college there together. Their parents knew each other and were extremely close. Dr. Garcia called Draven's mother Mom, and to him, she was his second mother. He did the same to Draven's father and was a pallbearer at his funeral.

Prior to attending San Francisco State University together, Draven and Dr. Garcia attended grammar school together. It was at this time that Ken befriended Draven and would become his closest, lifelong friend. Draven had a traumatic childhood, and he held a lot of anger inside because of it. He felt alone and experienced tremendous difficulties managing the daily psychological trauma from the scars of it. Ken had been a friend when Draven needed one desperately and did not have any. Through their friendship, Ken taught Draven many valuable lessons that he could not learn on his own. The most important was the ability to love oneself despite conditioned self- hatred from a sociopath. For that, Ken was called brother by Draven and held a deep place in his heart. Draven viewed Ken not only as a friend but as a brother. He was a guardian angel who was sent over to protect him. They had been through everything together and were friends until the end.

Draven entered Ken's residence. It was a massive mansion in the Seacliff District. A red Ferrari was parked in the driveway, and a black gate surrounded the residence. A pool was visible next to a basketball court toward the back of the building. Clearly, Ken was thriving in his practice and finally made it. A huge Filipino flag stood on a flagpole in front of his residence. Ken had never forgotten his roots and was extremely proud to be of Filipino ancestry.

They were both fiercely competitive with one another and loved friendly competition. This became evident when Ken brought the Madden PS4 video game out, and they were getting ready to play it. Each selected their team of choice, and they both wanted to be the San Francisco 49ERS, but a compromise was reached quickly. Within seconds, the game started, and the competition was fierce. The language became colorful, and voices were raised. When it was done, calmness was restored, and Draven congratulated Ken on his victory.

Suddenly, Draven saw the clock, and it said six o'clock. He told Ken that he needed to get going. He had tickets for the Siouxsie and the Banshee concert later today at 9:00 p.m. in the Warfield theater. Draven wanted to leave early because of the traffic. People left work at five, and he could be stuck in it for hours. This could cause Draven to miss the concert, and he did not want to take that chance. He also planned to eat dinner before going to the concert. After saying goodbye to Ken, Draven made arrangements for Uber to transport him to it. Within seconds, the Uber driver came, and Draven was on his way to the concert.

CHAPTER 13

The Uber driver dropped off Draven in front of the Warfield theater. Before going into it, he went to a nearby pizzeria. Draven ordered a slice of pepperoni pizza and sat down to eat it. While eating the pizza, he could feel the mixture of pepperoni, cheese, and tomato sauce enveloping his senses. His taste buds were in heaven, and he decided to take a small walk around the neighborhood before heading back to the Warfield theater for the upcoming concert. He walked through market street and noticed all the different shops that surrounded the area.

They sold products that ranged from incense to female hair care. Draven went into several of the stores and decided to sample some of the incense. He especially liked the Egyptian Musk fragrance and made plans to come back tomorrow to purchase it at one of the stores. It was getting late, and Draven decided to check the time on his cell phone. It said 7:40 p.m., so he proceeded to walk back to the Warfield theater.

Draven made it back to the Warfield theater and presented his ticket to the doorman. He noticed that Pit Bull Feliciano was handling security for the show tonight. They started talking, and Pit Bull informed Draven that he ran his own private security firm. It was called Pit Bull Enterprises and based out of San Francisco. He had offices in Los Angeles, Las Vegas, and New York. Pit Bull was a multimillionaire and did some security work for free. Sometimes, this included security at rock concerts for bands such as AC/DC, the Rolling Stones, and Bad Company. He loved rock concerts and everything about them.

Pit Bull was born and raised in the streets. He had a brutal childhood filled with massive psychological trauma. Draven befriended this individual several years ago and wanted to give Pit Bull the gift of undying friendship. He had experienced trauma that was similar to Pit Bull, and they both had massive psychological scars, which had been hidden for a long time. Pit Bull was the last of the badasses and outlaws. He loved playing chess with Draven because it gave his mind-mental stimulation. They had been friends for several years, and Pit Bull always looked out for Draven because of a promise that was made a long time ago. Pit Bull was a former marine sniper, and his word meant everything. It was his bond.

Draven said goodbye to Pit Bull and entered the ground floor of the concert hall. It was dark and difficult to see at times. There were wall- to-wall gothic faces, makeup, and piercings. He could see people wearing Siouxsie and the Banshees T-shirts, smoking weed, and having drinks while waiting for the show to begin. He found a seat near the front of the stage and looked out at the sea of humanity. They were his people, and he was at home.

The lights dimmed, and the Banshees came out on stage. People started screaming and smoke began to fill it. From nowhere, Siouxsie burst onto the stage, and the crowd went crazy. She belted out the lyrics to "Fireworks" and "Spellbound." Draven made eye contact with a goth girl at the concert, and he started dancing with her. She was beautiful and drop-dead gorgeous. This individual had long black hair and was wearing a Siouxsie and the Banshee T-shirt. They danced together for the entire concert and exchanged numbers. When it was over, she said her name was Roxie, and Draven could tell that she wanted to see him again. Even though Draven was madly in love with Asia Francisco, this lady had also caught his eye. The concert ended, and Draven vowed to call her later in the week. Before leaving the Warfield theater, he purchased his genuine Siouxsie and the Banshee T-shirt.

CHAPTER 14

Roxie left the concert and was ecstatic that she had met someone. She was on cloud nine and could not wait to see Draven again. Roxie was walking toward the BART station on 7th @ Market. She went inside and prepared to buy a ticket. It was eerily quiet at the BART station. She usually heard homeless people screaming expletives toward another person or police making an arrest. The only activity tonight appeared to be a group of homeless people using meth at the front entrance of the BART station. After purchasing her ticket, Roxie boarded the train and headed to Daly City.

She was shocked by the appearance of the train. The inside of the train was clean, and this eased her apprehension about having a seat in it. The train was not crowded, and this let her mind relax. She did not have to worry about talking to another individual. Roxie's feet were exhausted from a long night of partying, and she looked forward to soaking them in warm water with Epsom salt. She took a short nap and woke up to "Last Stop, Daly City." Roxie exited the train and proceeded to leave the station. She took out a small knife so that nobody would harm her as she walked to her car. As added protection, her phone was on and 911 predialed. She was ready to hit it when an emergency arose. Roxie had her car keys out.

Roxie thought about being able to soak her sore, tired feet in Epsom salt. She was getting lost in this thought as she approached her car. She hit the button on her key chain to unlock the car and proceeded to grab the door handle. From nowhere, she felt a huge blow to the back of her head and passed out. Roxie was placed in a van, and it sped off. This was the last time that she was ever seen alive again.

CHAPTER 15

Julie and her mother were set to go to the park today. It was a beautiful Sunday morning, and the hummingbirds were singing. The sun was shining, and a slight breeze permeated the air. The weather was perfect for a picnic at the park. Before heading to it, Julie and her mother packed various items needed for the picnic. These items included peanut butter and jelly sandwiches, chocolate cake, potato chips, sodas, sliced watermelon, paper plates, and napkins. There was some discussion regarding the type of soda that would be brought to the picnic, and both of them decided on Mug Root Beer. Additional items brought for the picnic included sunglasses, two hats, blankets, kites, and a bubble-blowing kit. Once everything was packed and loaded into the car, they headed to the park for a day of fun.

Traffic was light today, and they were at the park in fifteen minutes. Julie's mother could not believe that they made it to the park in such a short time. It was a three-day weekend, and traffic could be a nightmare because of this. Upon arriving at the park, they both noticed that it seemed quiet today. Normally, the park was bustling with activity on a three-day weekend. Julie's mother said, "At least we have the park to ourselves."

The park was located on Fourth/Brannon Street in San Francisco. It was created in the 1960s as a hideaway from the chaos known as humanity. Local politicians thought that life was becoming extremely hectic, and they felt that people needed a respite from the daily grind of stress, which resulted in the creation of the park. It took a massive amount of effort from different individuals, but eventually, this task was completed. The only stipulation was alcohol and drugs could not be used at the park. They wanted to keep it peaceful, safe, and relaxing at the park.

After making this selection, Julie's mother went to unload several items from the car. These items were going to be used for the picnic. She brought them to the area where the picnic would take place shortly. Julie's mother put the blanket on the grass and began preparing the food for consumption. This made her mouth water in anticipation of the upcoming feast.

While Julie's mother was preparing the food, Julie went to explore different areas of the park. She discovered a small pond where the ducks were squawking and splashing water at each other. Julie noticed that some of the ducks appeared different from one another. Some of the ducks had brown feathers all over their bodies. Others had a mixture of green and white feathers. She thought they were beautiful and could not stop gazing at the glorious tapestry of plumage that lay before her. While doing this, she noticed a squirrel run across the grass. He was moving very fast and appeared to be engaged in a flurry of activity. The squirrel was attempting to grab an acorn and bring it up the tree that he currently resided in. Eventually, he accomplished this task and decided to rest his weary body.

From the corner of her eye, Julie saw a shiny, silvery object and began approaching it. Julie attempted to grab the object, and while doing this, a human hand popped out. She screamed and ran back to her mother. Julie brought her mother to this spot, and she said, "Oh my god."

Julie's mother called the police, and they were there in minutes, but it felt like an eternity.

CHAPTER 16

The police came and sealed off the area. The forensics unit started taking pictures of the dead body from different angles. They began checking the plastic that the body was covered in for possible fingerprints. Asia Francisco gathered soil samples for examination and approached the dead body that was covered entirely in plastic. She took out her portable fingerprinting kit and grabbed one of the deceased's fingers. Asia placed it on the portable fingerprinting scanner. The fingerprint was taken and stored in the scanner for later examination. When done, Asia placed the finger back under the plastic covering.

A police officer approached Julie and introduced himself as Officer Garcia. He spoke initially to Julie's mother, and she granted him permission to talk to her daughter. Julie's mother informed Officer Garcia that she wanted to be present when he spoke to her daughter. Officer Garcia agreed to this, and he escorted both of them to a quieter area of the park. After doing this, Julie recounted the details surrounding the discovery of the deceased to Officer Garcia. When done, the police officer handed Julie's mother a business card with his name and contact information on it. He told both of these individuals to remain at the crime scene because Detective Overstreet may have additional questions for them. Officer Garcia informed Julie and her mother that this individual was the detective assigned to the case.

Draven arrived on the scene and parked his car. Officer Garcia proceeded to escort Draven to the crime scene where the dead body was located. The dead body appeared to be that of a Caucasian female in her mid-thirties. It was covered completely in plastic, and the victim's clothes were missing. The dead body was devoid of color as if all the blood had been drained from it. A puncture wound was present on the back of each arm and leg.

The dead body had tattoos on it. One was a picture of Siouxsie Sioux from Siouxsie and the Banshees. It was on her left arm. The other ones were on the right arm, and they said, "Born to raise hell," along with "Gothic for life." The victim had a piercing on the left side of her nose. Her right ear was completely covered with piercings. The body was placed in a very peaceful position, and it looked as if she was sleeping.

While examining the dead body, Draven thought that this person looked familiar. He could not remember where he knew this individual from. While looking at the Siouxsie and the Banshee tattoo on her left arm, he remembered that she was the woman he danced with while at the Siouxsie and the Banshee concert last night. He did not recognize her because he had never seen this individual naked and without makeup before.

While lost in his own thoughts, Draven noticed that Asia Francisco was approaching the crime scene. Asia informed Draven that she already obtained fingerprints of the deceased. She talked about using her portable fingerprinting scanner to do this. She brought her notebook out and proceeded to review the details of the crime scene with Draven. They included appearance, location, and position of the dead body upon initial discovery. Other details included gender and age of the deceased. Additional ones pertained to presence of tattoos and piercings on the body.

CHAPTER 17

When done talking to Julie and her mother, he went to look for Asia. Draven wanted to continue the conversation that he attempted to have with her earlier. He found Asia looking at the plastic covering that the dead body was covered in.

Draven's heart was beating a mile a minute. He finally had a chance to speak to Forensic Expert Asia Francisco alone. Draven had waited forever for this moment, but he needed to maintain focus on the issue at hand. There was a killer plaguing the city, and they did not have a clue who this person was. They did not have a lot of evidence to go on, and there was no pattern behind the selection of the victims. They appeared to be so random.

Draven began speaking to Asia. "What do you have so far?"

The victims vary on age. Some are in their twenties, and others in their thirties. They all had different jobs, and none of them are related. The highest form of education completed ranged from high school to college. They lived in various parts of the Bay Area, but all the bodies were found in San Francisco. That was another factor that tied them all together. Asia added, "The fingerprints came back for each victim." Their names were Trish Armstrong, Lisa Miranda, and Roxie Youngblood."

Draven listened as Asia relayed some information she discovered when examining the bodies. All the bodies had four puncture wounds —one on the back of each arm and leg. These puncture wounds were medium-sized, and a tube could fit in each of them. Asia thought this would explain the bodies being drained of all their blood. She knew from past cases that this was a possibility and wanted to look into it.

Draven was stumped and did not know where a killer would purchase tubes that would be used to drain the blood from a human being. Detective Overstreet was not sure how much they would cost. He gathered that they could be expensive and thought that the killer came from a rich family. But still there was no way to confirm this, which further irritated, frustrated, and enraged Draven. He desperately wanted to catch this killer and put an end to his carnage.

Draven almost became lost in his own thoughts, but Asia was able to pull him out of this. Draven's stomach started growling, and he decided to go to Vees for lunch. He asked Asia to come with him, and she said yes. At the restaurant, Draven ordered two hamburgers with french fries. One of them was for Asia. He was hungry and devoured his meal in seconds. Asia was surprised and had never seen anyone eat a meal this quickly before. She gathered that Draven had been starving and could not hold back his appetite any longer. When done eating, Draven asked quietly to himself, *Did I even taste it?*

CHAPTER 18

The killer muttered to himself, *Another day at the office and so much paperwork to complete*. He wondered if it ever stopped. The killer thought about this daily at work. He watched the long lines of customers waiting for assistance, and he felt relieved that his lunch break had finally arrived. The killer loved his deli sandwiches and would often go to Sweet Chinitos for lunch. Sweet Chinitos was a deli located in Mission Street. It had the best ham sandwiches in San Francisco, and the price was reasonable. He had the deli worker put everything on it, except pimiento. It was too spicey and caused indigestion. He had a root beer with his ham sandwich and a chocolate chip cookie for dessert.

While eating his sandwich, the killer read an article from the datebook section of the *San Francisco Chronicle*. It focused on the latest movies that were playing in various theaters throughout San Francisco. The article gave a summary and a review of different films. The killer wondered how a producer spent millions of dollars on a movie that turned out to be total garbage. He pondered to himself, *Are they aware when this is happening? Probably not.*

The killer decided to stop reading about this and proceeded to put the datebook section of the newspaper away. He slowly ate his sandwich and enjoyed every minute of it. The ham was shaved perfectly, and the roll baked to perfection. The roll was extremely crunchy, and the pickle that came with the sandwich was very crispy. The brine accented the taste of the pickle perfectly. When the killer was done, he ate the chocolate chip cookie and finished drinking his Mug Root Beer. The killer thanked the deli worker for making a delicious sandwich that was truly a work of art. Before walking out of the deli, he smiled at this person and placed a five-dollar bill in the tip bottle.

He exited the deli and proceeded to walk back to work. The killer smiled and thought to himself, *Did that person realize that they just served a monster? Did the world realize they had a monster hiding in plain sight?* The killer muttered "Probably not, but I think very little of humanity."

CHAPTER 19

"This is Allysa Collins, and welcome to Channel 7 News. The police have no leads as to the identity of the serial killer plaguing San Francisco. They cannot find any connection between the victims. The victims range in age and were found in different locations throughout San Francisco. The only things connecting them is their gender and the fact that these dead bodies had been discovered in San Francisco."

Draven listened to this segment of the news and turned the channel once it was over. He changed it to ESPN and proceeded to watch the Golden State Warrior basketball game. They were winning, and Stephen Curry appeared to be on fire. His three-point shooting was out of sight today, and he was on pace to score forty points tonight. They were facing the San Antonio Spurs. Draven watched Coach Kerr patrol his side of the court and saw that the coach for the San Antonio Spurs was doing the same. It was a close game, but the Warriors won in the end. Draven watched as the two coaches hugged each other and congratulated each other on a well-played game. They had been friends for years and respected one another. Gregg Popovich gave Steve Kerr his start as a coach. For that, he was extremely grateful.

When it was over, he put on a horror movie and passed out from exhaustion. Little Jimmi did the same. Horror movies seemed to relax Draven, and he could never figure out why. He thought about this before, and the only explanation could be that horror movies tapped into some deep, psychological trauma that was trapped in his mind that needed releasing. Horror movies appeared to provide this release in a safe and comfortable environment.

CHAPTER 20

Draven turned on the television set and went to the kitchen to make his coffee. When going to the kitchen, he could hear the reporter from CNN talking about the state of the country: more bad news about the economy, various wars in different far-off countries, and the never- ending hate crimes along with shootings, which continued to plague the United States like cancer. Draven often wondered why he started each day watching national news because it was so damn depressing and if one listened to it long enough, they could feel their faith in humanity slowly dying.

Draven finished making his coffee and retrieved a donut. He sat down. Before doing this, Little Jimmi came to greet him with his morning loves. Draven got Little Jimmi from the SPCA three weeks ago, and Little Jimmi was only eight weeks old. Little Jimmi was a labrador, pit bull, and terrier mix. He had a massive streak of white fur that stretched from Little Jimmi's butt to his neck and was the cutest dog that you ever saw. Little Jimmi loved Draven and greeted him with licks on his cheek. While reading about this behavior in several books pertaining to the psychology of dogs, Draven discovered that the licks on the cheek were the equivalency of kisses that human beings gave to one another as a sign of affection.

They both sat on the floor and proceeded to eat breakfast together. Little Jimmi was done with his breakfast in five minutes and was ready to play. He started jumping up and down, which indicated that Little Jimmi was ready to play. Before doing that, Draven turned off the television set. He played several games with Little Jimmi, which included Man Vs. Dog and Battle Royal. This was one of their favorite parts of the day. They both wished that it would never end, but Draven had to go to work, so he could be able to continue to care for Little Jimmi.

When done playing with Little Jimmi, Draven showered and proceeded to get ready for work. He picked out his Siouxsie and the Banshees T-shirt and black jeans and put them on. Before dressing, he turned the channel to the local news, where the mayor was seen giving a press conference. He talked about the serial killer on the loose in the city and told the press that a suspect had not been identified. The mayor stated that he had no leads pertaining to this and that police were working around the clock to provide the killer's name.

Draven started thinking to himself, *We have no leads as to the identity of the killer. We are working around the clock and are not even close to solving the case. The victims have nothing in common, except their gender, and they appear to be selected so randomly. Draven could feel himself being overwhelmed with stress and almost became lost in his own thoughts.*

Draven heard a knock on the door. He approached it and asked, "Who's there?" Draven knew that he could not be too careful because of the constant violence that plagued certain areas of San Francisco. He heard a voice say, "Maria Vega, and I am here to take Little Jimmi back to my apartment while you go to work." Maria was Draven's neighbor, and they had known each other for several years. She was currently taking flamenco dance classes at San Francisco State University. Someday, she hoped to work at one of the premier dance studios in Spain. In the meantime, Maria supplemented her income by watching Little Jimmi while Draven was at work. She could use the extra money due to the rising costs of tuition and textbooks.

Draven presented Little Jimmi to Maria. Little Jimmi started barking and had the saddest eyes in the world when leaving Draven. He wanted Draven to stay with him but knew that his owner had to go to work. This was the saddest part of the day for Draven, and it never got easier. Little Jimmi eventually calmed down, and Maria was able to take him to her apartment.

CHAPTER 21

Before proceeding to work, he stopped at the crime lab to talk to Asia Francisco about her report pertaining to the case. Draven approached Asia and listened as she talked about details she uncovered about the case. She stated that the bodies did not have any fingerprints or hair fibers on them. Asia said that signs of sexual assault or abuse were not present on the bodies. The one thing that stood out was that each body had the odor of methamphetamine, which seemed to permeate in their pores. The women themselves did not have a history of drug abuse or addiction. They did not live in a neighborhood where there was heavy drug usage.

The women did not have any signs of a struggle on their bodies. They were all in great shape and did not have any medical issues. They did not have a history of mental illness and looked healthy. Asia Francisco read over statements gathered by the police at the crime scene from people who knew the victims. They were described as hardworking, kind, and gentle souls who lived and enjoyed life and wanted to give back to the community. Some of them even volunteered at the local SPCA during the weekends, and all had a close circle of friends who could not believe what had happened. Draven decided that this could possibly be a good starting point.

It took Draven several days to track down close friends of the victims. He talked to them about their fallen friends and obtained information, but he still did not have anything which connected the victims. The only thing that they shared in common was that they were females between the ages of twenty and thirty-five and who either attended San Francisco State University in the past or graduated from it. Draven was already stumped by this case and wondered if he would ever obtain information that connected the victims. The only things that he knew were that the victims were piling up and he still did not have a clue as to the identity of the killer, but he decided to look into another area of interest, which would be attendance records at San Francisco State University. He decided that he would speak to the president of San Francisco State University before talking to some of the students and examining attendance records of the victims.

CHAPTER 22

Detective Draven Overstreet went to the president's office at San Francisco State University. It was located behind Burk Hall in the administration building. When approaching the building, he could see that the students were looking at him. He could tell that this individual looked mysterious and they did not recognize him. They were all probably asking who he was and why he was on campus. If you are on campus long enough, people would recognize you, and Draven thought that the other students were wondering who this blue-eyed stranger was.

While walking to the administrative building, he started to remember his time attending San Francisco State University. He remembered the long walks to get to his classes and the insane amount of money spent at the bookstore for textbooks. Draven recalled the numerous rallies that were held for various causes at San Francisco State University. These included the ongoing struggle for Israeli/Palestine rights, LGBT rights, antiwar marches especially when the second war in Iraq started, and the continued struggle for environmental justice. He remembered the flag that he created to unify the hetero along with LGBT worlds it signified and the struggle he became personally involved with pertaining to gay marriage. Draven remembered the first love he had while all this was happening, someone he met before graduating from this university, along with the breakup that followed a year later. These memories were an inch thick, but he brushed them off his mind to focus on the task at hand.

Draven reached the administrative building and was exhausted by the time he got to it. It was a long walk, but he made it. He noticed the building had a new paint job and a new coffee kiosk placed right outside it. He bought an herbal tea and drank it while taking in the sights and sounds of the university. Draven watched all the different students walking around the building. He even noticed that some of the female students were staring at him with those eyes requesting that he talk to them. Once he was done drinking his tea, he decided to go talk to the president of the school before the tea put him to sleep.

CHAPTER 23

Detective Overstreet entered the administrative building and checked to see which floor the president's office was located at. He noticed that it was on the third floor, so he took an elevator up. Draven got off on the third floor and headed to the president's office. Upon entering, he noticed that he had to be buzzed in by his assistant before speaking to the president. Draven flashed his badge, and he informed her that he needed to speak to the president of the university about an urgent police matter. He could tell that the administrative assistant was startled but intrigued and possibly turned on by his appearance. He wasn't wearing the normal suit, slacks, and tie, which were the traditional uniform of choice for a detective. Draven also had numerous rings on his fingers and piercings, which did not fit the normal attire of a San Francisco Police Department detective. But his supervisor, had given him a pass on his appearance because of his great police skills and huge clearance rate on cases.

He spoke to the president's administrative assistant, and she proceeded to buzz him in. Once in the office, the president introduced himself to Draven, and Draven shook his hand. He noticed brown with tan-colored chairs and desks inside it. Draven also saw a framed autographed picture of former president Barack Obama on the wall. He noticed that the president of the school had a framed certificate of his master's degree in business administration from the University of California in Berkley.

President Corrigan invited Det. Draven Overstreet to sit down. Draven talked about the serial killer that was on the loose in San Francisco and informed the president of the connection between the university and some victims. He said that some had graduated from the university, while others were currently attending it. Draven presented the names of these students to the president and told him that he wanted to talk to their friends and professors. Draven did not want to alarm the students on campus with a police presence, so he hoped that the president could help him with this. President Corrigan was alarmed and concerned about the university's connection to the murders, and Draven could see that he was worried about the safety of the current student body.

With Draven in the office, President Corrigan contacted the editor of the school newspaper via telephone about this. He informed the editor that a special edition of the newspaper needed to be created to alert the students about this latest development. Draven thought that this was a great idea and suggested that he speak to the head of campus security to make them aware of the situation. President Corrigan contacted head of campus security via telephone and requested that this individual come to the president's office. He was there in several minutes, and Draven made him aware of the situation.

In the background, Draven heard President Corrigan cancel night classes until the killer was apprehended. He advised the editor of the school newspaper to place this notice in the special edition, which would hit newsstands later today. President Corrigan also said that he would have a press release later today with the media to relay this information to the public.

Toward the end of their meeting, Draven presented the names of the students that he would be talking to the president. Draven informed the president that he would be checking the attendance of these students. He wanted to see if there were any attendance abnormalities.

CHAPTER 24

Detective Overstreet was given a picture of Harley Carmichael by the president of the university. He was told that she was currently in her abnormal psychology class in Burk Hall and that it would end at one thirty. He looked at his watch and noticed that it would be forty-five minutes from now. He watched as the president of the university gave Detective Overstreet her school file so he could gain more information about her. Detective Overstreet saw that Harley was a Caucasian female majoring in psychology. This was her second year at the university, and she was born in San Francisco. He saw that she was twenty-five years old and lived on campus. He thanked the president of the university for letting him look at the file before returning it.

Detective Overstreet then went to Burk Hall to speak to Harley Carmichael. He waited several minutes for the class to end. When he saw her exit the classroom, Detective Overstreet approached her. He took out his badge and introduced himself. He could see that she was nervous and uncomfortable. He said that he wanted to talk to her about the murder of her friend. She said that she would be willing to do this but would not do it in campus. She arranged to meet Detective Overstreet at Starbucks in Stonestown Mall later that day at four. Draven agreed and decided to take care of some additional errands before meeting Harley later.

While speaking with Harley in the hall, he noticed that she wore mostly black. She was wearing a black skirt and a T-shirt. Her hair was black with red highlights. She had piercings on her nose and in both ears. Harley had several rings in her fingers, and she was wearing boots. She had makeup on her face, and he could tell that this person was part of the Gothic subculture.

CHAPTER 25

Detective Overstreet arrived at four o'clock in Starbucks for his meeting with Harley Carmichael. She was not there yet. He waited several minutes for her to arrive. She was there at four fifteen and had not changed her clothing since their initial meeting.

Detective Overstreet reintroduced himself to Harley and thanked her for her assistance in this matter. Detective Overstreet said that he was sorry for her loss. He then proceeded to ask Harley about the nature of her relationship with the deceased. He listened and watched as Harley talked about meeting Trisha when they were children. Harley spoke about Trish being her best friend whom she shared many experiences with. She recounted some of these experiences. Detective Overstreet then asked Harley about her whereabouts the day of the murder, and he listened as she talked about being in class all day. Then Harley talked about going home after class and falling asleep due to it being a long day. After that, Detective Overstreet asked Harley about any arguments she had with Trisha prior to her murder, and she responded by saying, "We did not have any arguments or fights when I saw her last. We were actually planning to go to a concert over the weekend, and now that won't be happening."

Detective Overstreet could see that this questioning was starting to upset Harley. Her face was red, and her voice was beginning to crack. Tears were starting to stream down her face, smearing her makeup, and she needed a break from this line of questioning. Detective Overstreet thanked Harley for her cooperation in this matter and apologized for upsetting her. He sent his condolences to Harley, again pertaining to her loss, and watched as she exited the coffee shop.

He ordered an orange zinger to calm his nerves after the questioning was over. He could see that Harley was upset by the questioning and felt bad about it. He did not like retraumatizing individuals who lost loved ones by having to ask them questions about it. This was a part of the job that he hated, and he was happy that it was over. With that, he drank his orange zinger and enjoyed the soothing, relaxing inner peace that the tea provided. Tea calmed his nerves when needed. It was something he learned a long time ago.

CHAPTER 26

He went in and spoke to the manager at the restaurant. He was a male of Asian descent named Ron and had been working at the restaurant since it opened in 1994. Detective Overstreet asked questions pertaining to Trish's work performance. The manager said that Trish was a hardworking, conscientious employee who worked hard and always showed up on time and ready to work. They also talked about Trish's relationships with the customers and other employees. Ron said that Trish got along great with the customers and other employees at the restaurant. He said that everyone loved Trish, and he described her as having a warm, generous heart and a great personality. Ron said, "I hope that someone catches this animal," when questioning was completed.

Detective Overstreet thanked Ron for his time and cooperation in this matter. Detective Overstreet apologized for any stress and emotional pain that this brought up for him. He could tell that this questioning upset Ron deeply, and he again felt bad about this. He could tell that Ron really cared about and looked after Trish as if she was his own daughter.

Detective Overstreet exited the restaurant and proceeded to walk to his car. He reviewed Ron's answers internally to the questions that he asked him and thought that it was a dead end. He did not obtain any new information about Trish that could help him identify and locate her killer.

CHAPTER 27

Detective Overstreet went to see Asia Francisco in the forensics lab to talk more about the case with her. While driving to the lab, he wondered how she was doing and was anxious to talk to her about the case and other matters. He could feel himself getting excited about the possibility of talking to her. He often wondered, *Was she aware that I liked her?*

He finally reached the building where the forensics lab was located. Detective Overstreet parked his car and noticed that he was able to get a parking spot in front of the building. He entered the building and proceeded to the basement where the forensics lab was located. Before entering the lab, he could hear Siouxsie and the Banshees playing inside it.

Detective Overstreet entered and saw that Asia Francisco was deep in thought and did not notice him. She turned around and jumped when she saw him. Asia was startled and said, "Next time, Draven put a bell on."

Detective Overstreet started laughing and said, "Is that Siouxsie and the Banshees playing?"

"Yes," replied Asia.

Detective Overstreet started talking about the Siouxsie and the Banshee concert that he attended last week. He also noticed that incense was burning in the background.

Asia told him, "It's called dragon magic."

Detective Overstreet said, "I like the fragrance."

"It's sold in an incense shop on Columbus Street in San Francisco," Asia mentioned.

They talked for hours before Draven remembered why he initially decided to come to see Asia Francisco. He found himself completely attracted to her and loved everything about her, especially her physical appearance. He dreamed of slow dancing with Asia Francisco and taking her to a hill off the coast of San Francisco and kissing her as the sun went down. He knew that if he was able to get her alone and show her his world, she would fall in love with him and be forever his.

Detective Overstreet told himself that he needed to focus on the case, despite the sexual passion that was brewing deep inside him for Asia Francisco. He began talking about the case and described the steps that he was taking to solve it. He spoke about the individuals he talked to about the case and about being unable to obtain any leads as to the identity of the killer and voiced his frustration about the case to her.

Asia noticed that Detective Overstreet was beginning to become uptight and irritated the more he talked about the case. She put her arms around his back and started to massage it. She noticed that he was starting to relax the more she did this, and Detective Overstreet asked her to continue to do this.

While doing this, Draven started to become aroused and saw that it was time to go. He could feel the sexual passion stirring within him and taking control of his body. He wanted to take Asia, throw her on the floor, and ravage her, and he could see that Asia felt the same way.

With that, they gave in completely to the lust they felt toward one another and went at it like wild beasts on a warm, summer night. Asia grabbed Detective Overstreet's love wand and began sucking it like someone taking the chrome off a car. He then rubbed his steel cannon over her while she moaned and howled with excitement. They were truly howling at the moon, and this would be a night that they would never forget.

CHAPTER 28

Detective Overstreet left Asia Francisco's lab a changed man. He felt so relaxed in many ways and walked to his car with renewed vigor. Detective Overstreet had cemented his relationship with Asia Francisco and had said and expressed his deep love for her. He had held it in for many years and now was happy that it was out in the open.

Detective Overstreet went home and decided to check on his dog. While driving home, he noticed that traffic was light and made it to his apartment in twenty minutes. He went to retrieve his dog, Little Jimmi (his loyal companion and best friend), and thanked his neighbor for watching him and then brought him home.

Detective Overstreet made a list of the people he wanted to speak to regarding the unsolved murders. When done, he looked it over and decided on his next course of action. He decided that the next person he wanted to speak to was Eliza Barclay, the best friend and roommate of the recently deceased Lisa Miranda.

CHAPTER 29

Before going to speak to Eliza about the recent murder of her best friend, he decided that he needed to speak to the president of the University of San Francisco first. Detective Overstreet recently discovered that Lisa and Eliza were best friends and roommates. He needed access to Lisa Miranda's school records and had to get permission from the president in order to do this. He also wanted permission from the president to speak to Eliza Barclay about the murder of her best friend. Plus, he knew that the police were going to be on campus to talk to other people about the unsolved murder of a student, and the president needed to be aware of this. He decided that this would take place on Monday morning.

It was Saturday morning, and Detective Overstreet decided that he wanted to spend the day with his dog. They went to Baker Beach. He watched as Little Jimmi played in the sand and water. Draven noticed that the wet water never seemed to bother Little Jimmi. It was as though it relaxed him. He watched as Little Jimmi played with the other dogs and seemed to be having a great time. It was a dog's life for sure.

CHAPTER 30

On Monday, Detective Overstreet went to see the president of the University of San Francisco. It was a long journey due to the heavy traffic, and Draven started to wish that he did this at another time. He arrived at the building that housed the president's office in thirty-five minutes. The building was a tall cream-colored structure that was covered with moss on one side. He parked his car and proceeded to enter it. Draven saw that the president's office was on the third floor, so he took the elevator to it. It was a long ordeal to get to the office, and Draven almost passed out before getting there. He forgot how much walking it took to get to certain offices at the University of San Francisco.

Detective Overstreet arrived at the president's office. He entered the office and noticed that a waiting room stood before it. He saw that a receptionist's desk was outside the president's office. She asked him to have a seat because she was on the phone. When done with her call, she asked Detective Overstreet, "How could I help you?" Draven introduced himself as Detective Overstreet from the San Francisco Police Department and talked about needing to speak to the president of the university about a police matter. Draven waited as the receptionist contacted the president via telephone and explained the situation to him. The receptionist told him that he could go in, and Draven thanked her for her assistance.

Draven entered the president's office and saw him sitting behind a desk. His back was turned to Draven, and he was talking to someone on the phone. Draven noticed that it was a small office with a modest amount of furniture in it. He saw that the president of the university had several pictures with the pope and himself on the wall. He also noticed a college diploma on the wall, which stated that he graduated with a degree in theology from the University of San Francisco in 1990. He also noticed a metal cross and several framed autographed pictures of the president with several athletes, which included Stephen Curry along with Tom Brady.

When the president turned around to face Draven after ending his call, Draven saw that he was a priest. The president introduced himself as Fr. Fitzgerald to Draven and talked about wanting to cooperate with the police regarding whatever business brought him to the university. Father Fitzgerald was a tall, skinny, older Caucasian male. He had gray, silver hair and was wearing a Roman collar along with his cleric suit. He was clean-shaven and appeared to be in good shape.

Detective Overstreet thanked Fr. Fitzgerald for his cooperation and introduced himself to him. Draven mentioned that he graduated from the University in 2007 and had many fond memories of it, which included attending numerous college basketball games as well as swimming in its Olympic-sized pool.

He then talked about the recent murder of a student from this university and requested to see her file to gain more information pertaining to a possible motive. He said the victim's name was Lisa Miranda. Detective Overstreet could tell that the president was in shock about the murder of Lisa Miranda. Draven watched as the president could barely speak and had to sit down. The only things he said were, "I spoke to her last week and she was excited about the upcoming dance for new incoming students." Detective Overstreet listened as Father Fitzgerald talked about Lisa serving on the committee to organize the dance because she was from another state and knew how homesick and lonely some out-of-state students became when leaving home for the first time. Father Fitzgerald went on to say "she was such a nice, giving soul, and I pray that you find her killer. A soul like that deserves justice and to be at rest forever."

Draven also informed Fr. Fitzgerald that the murdered

victim's best friend, Eliza Barclay, went to the same university and he needed to see her school file also. Father Fitzgerald granted Draven permission to see the file that it was in the Bursar's office. Draven indicated that he knew where the Bursar's office was and thanked the president for his cooperation in this matter.

CHAPTER 31

Detective Overstreet went to go speak to Eliza Barclay about the recent death of her friend. While reviewing her file, he was able to see her class schedule and saw that she had art appreciation at one in Phelan Hall. Draven started walking to Phelan Hall and headed to room 101 in that building. He arrived five minutes before class let out. He noticed that he had five minutes to wait before Eliza's class let out and decided to check his email.

The door swung open in the classroom designed for the art appreciation class, and Eliza Barclay exited. Eliza was on her cell phone and making plans to attend a party the following night at ten. It was supposed to be the biggest party of the year, and Eliza was determined to attend it.

Detective Overstreet approached Eliza and introduced himself to her. He flashed his badge and said that he wanted to talk to her about the recent death of her friend. She talked about wanting to do it later today in the cafeteria at two. Draven agreed and noticed that this was forty-nine minutes from now. He let Eliza go and decided that he needed to eat something before their meeting about the murder of her friend.

Detective Overstreet went to The Blue and Gold Room in the university. He ordered a hamburger, along with fries and a Mug root beer. Draven was starving and finished his lunch in twenty minutes. He was surprised by this and underestimated his level of hunger. He thought to himself, *This food was as good as ever*. It was also still reasonable in price.

Draven waited in the cafeteria for Eliza Barclay. She was twenty minutes late and seemed to be flustered. Draven noticed that she had not changed her clothes since their impromptu meeting earlier today. Eliza was wearing blue jeans and a flannel. She was not wearing any makeup but had several rings on her fingers. Her clothes were wrinkled, and she was wearing a beanie on top of her head.

Detective Overstreet thanked Eliza for agreeing to see him and pulled up a chair for her. He gave condolences to Eliza pertaining to her recent loss, and he could tell that Eliza appreciated this. Draven asked about Lisa's mood since she last spoke to her. Eliza said that Lisa seemed frustrated because she wanted to go to Paris for spring break and was having difficulties obtaining the funds needed to make this happen. Draven asked questions pertaining to her relationship with Lisa Miranda, and Eliza said that she worried about Lisa not being able to secure the documents needed to obtain a passport for Paris, which included a California identification along with a Social Security card. Eliza talked about Lisa having problems managing stress with going to school, working, and completing her homework for classes. She also mentioned that Lisa seemed impatient with her at times and would yell at her when becoming overwhelmed with frustration pertaining to balancing work along with school-related responsibilities. Eliza said that Lisa needed a break from these responsibilities and saw the trip to Paris as a respite needed for recharging. She told Draven that Lisa was normally relaxed and happy-go-lucky. She also told him that Lisa was normally cool and a pleasure to interact with and something was clearly bothering her.

Eliza Barclay informed Detective Overstreet that she had to cut their meeting short as she had another class to attend. Detective Overstreet gave Eliza his business card and said that she could contact him with any additional information pertaining to the murder of Lisa Miranda. Draven made sure to put his cell phone number on this card before giving it to her. He thanked Eliza for her cooperation and watched as she proceeded to go to her class.

CHAPTER 32

Suzie and Ryan were getting ready for a jog at the beach. It was early Saturday morning, and the weekend was finally here. They were both nurses who worked at San Francisco General Hospital, and each one had a hectic schedule. They started out as friends and quickly became a couple. It had been love at first sight for them. They had been together for a year, and both agreed it was one of the best times of their lives. They recently adopted a dog, a beagle, who they named Aurora. They were going to take her to the beach with them.

They placed harness and leash on Aurora, which proved to be a frustrating and difficult experience, but they were able to accomplish this task. They left the house and proceeded to walk to the beach. The couple lived no more than five minutes away from the beach, so they could easily walk to it.

They arrived at the beach, which took them less time than expected. The beach was dog-friendly and not that busy today. The air was warm, and the sun was out. They detected a slight breeze in the air but not enough to warrant the use of a coat. The stage was set for a nice, relaxing day at the beach for both humans and dog.

Suzie took Aurora and proceeded to introduce her to the water at the beach. She had never felt it before, and the coldness of the water startled her. Suzie felt something brush against her leg and thought it was the dog reacting to the cold water. It happened again, and Suzie looked down to discover a dead body had washed up onshore. It touched her leg and startled her.

Ryan heard the scream and ran over. He saw that Suzie and Aurora were upset and shaking. He grabbed both of them and attempted to calm each one down. He then phoned the San Francisco Police Department to report the discovery of a dead body, and the dispatcher said authorities would be there soon.

CHAPTER 33

The police arrived at the scene and began to take a statement from Suzie. She talked about taking the dog to play in the beach and feeling something brush against her leg. She spoke about thinking it was her dog because he had never been to a beach before and the water had been cold, which caused him to jump earlier in the day. While talking about this with the police officer, she noticed that it was making her antsy, and she wanted to leave. Officer Garcia said he had a couple more questions and then he would let her go.

While the police officer was speaking to Suzie, crime scene investigators were busy gathering evidence. Asia Francisco was overseeing this effort, and she started having the body dusted for fingerprints. Asia had another technician scan the body for bruising along with puncture wounds that could be analyzed later. Soil samples were taken as well as photographs of the entire crime scene. While all this was happening, police officers kept nonessential personnel away from the crime scene to prevent contamination of evidence.

This proved to be an extremely difficult and challenging experience. Bystanders kept attempting to cross the yellow police tape and wanted to see the dead body. They were genuinely curious, and police had to constantly escort onlookers away from the crime scene. This interfered with crime scene investigators who were busy gathering evidence, and the threat of contamination loomed in the air because of this. The press also attempted to cross the yellow line and take pictures of the body. They had to be constantly kept away from the crime scene by the police, and it proved to be a nightmare.

Detective Overstreet arrived at the scene of the investigation. He heard it through his police scanner. Traffic was light, so he arrived there in twenty minutes. Officer Garcia presented him with the details of the crime and talked about the witnesses who had discovered the body.

Detective Overstreet thanked Officer Garcia for his information pertaining to the investigation. He proceeded to approach the witnesses and introduced himself to both Susie and Ryan, who recounted the experience of discovering the body. When they were done, Detective Overstreet gave them his business card and also thanked them for their assistance.

Draven then approached forensics expert Asia Francisco regarding her impressions of the case. She talked about needing to conduct further examination of the body to gather more evidence of the crime. She did tell him that they have a serial killer on their hands.

CHAPTER 34

It was a busy day at the office. The phones were ringing off the hook. The lines were long and complaints many. The customers would not stop coming, and workers were running around like chickens with their heads cut off. The hum of computers filled the air, and so did the cigarette smoke from the workers. It was a chaotic atmosphere full of constant activity.

Yet the killer kept on working. He was able to block out all the chaos around him and focus on a task that he was trying to complete on the computer. He could hear his supervisor yelling at him in the background, but he did not seem to give a shit. He thought to himself, *What a useless human being and a waste of life. She is too uptight and needs to get laid.* While deep in thought, he could see that his supervisor gave up trying to get his attention and went to do something else.

The killer could feel himself getting excited about tonight. He was going out hunting and had already selected his next victim.

CHAPTER 35

Roxie Garcia was excited about her first day at work in Mo Greens. She could hardly contain herself. This was her first job, and she had recently signed a lease for an apartment in San Francisco located on Ninth Street. It had a bathroom, kitchen, and shower inside it. It was a steal at $1,200 per month, and Roxie was grateful for this. Her friends were all paying $3,000 a month, and some of them lived in the dangerous area of town.

Roxie arrived at work early and met the other employees. She was given a tour of the shop but knew it well due to being a repeat customer. Roxie listened as her supervisor told her to scan IDs of anyone entering the shop before letting them speak to a salesperson. This helped ensure safety for everyone in the store and assisted with crowd control.

Roxie was busy all day and could not believe how fast the time went. It was four o'clock before she knew it, and it was time to go home. She said goodbye to her coworkers and proceeded to her car. Roxie drove a Ford Taurus and dreamed of the day that she could purchase a new car. As for now, she settled on being a broke college student trying to get by.

She walked around the corner of the shop to the parking lot, which was located at the back of Mo Greens. Roxie wished that she did not have to park in it. It was too isolated, and she felt that it presented to much of a danger to her overall safety. It was dimly lit at night and too confined for her.

As Roxie was getting closer to the parking lot, she took out her key and had it ready to open the car when she heard a noise and turned around. Nothing was there. She turned her head forward, and that was when he grabbed her. He put a handkerchief around her neck, which had alcohol soaked into it, and she passed out. It was all over that quickly. She was placed in a van and never seen and heard from again.

CHAPTER 36

The mayor looked outside his office window and could see the crowd gathering in the parking lot. There were hundreds of them led by an individual with a bullhorn. Some were carrying banners that said to impeach the mayor, while others were handing out flyers with the same message on them. It seemed to be getting larger and louder and was attracting a lot of attention from onlookers.

Reporters from Kron 4 News were outside and just finishing their coverage of another story. They came and saw that the crowd was upset and demanded that the mayor be impeached. A serial killer was on the loose, and they felt nothing was being done about it. The crowd continued to scream of demands of impeachment, and it reached a loud roar of frustration. The police started to come to see what the commotion was all about and began to worry about the safety of the mayor.

The mayor, meanwhile, was in his office, and he could hear everything that was happening outside. He decided that he needed to speak to the crowd in an attempt to quell the commotion. Some of the police decided to go outside with the mayor as a safety precaution. The mayor thought that by doing this, the crowd would calm down.

He went outside and decided to talk to the crowd. The reporters from Kron 4 News turned on their cameras, and Kron 4 News interrupted local programming. The mayor approached the news cameras and relayed the following message:

Good afternoon, fellow San Franciscans. A monster is on the loose in our city and targeting fellow San Franciscans. I know that you are scared and worried about the safety of your loved ones. I have authorized the police and the office of the district attorney to do everything possible to catch this monster. Overtime has been authorized and a curfew set in place. A task force is being created to find and apprehend this monster. People can no longer be out at night, and those violating it will be arrested. Everyone, be safe, and rest assured, we will bring this monster to justice.

CHAPTER 37

Detective Overstreet went to his favorite watering hole. It was called EZ5 and a staple of the neighborhood. The owner of the bar, who also tended it, was Bernie Shwartz. He was working today, and they had been childhood friends since the age of nine. They often joked about knowing each other better than their girlfriends ever would.

Detective Overstreet ordered his favorite drink (Grolsch, which was a caramel-flavored beer) and glanced up at the television set. The Golden State Warriors were playing the Los Angelos Clippers. They were beating the Los Angelos Clippers by a large amount, and this made Detective Overstreet smile. Draven never liked the Los Angelos Clippers because they engaged in trash talk, which made the game against them personal.

Draven asked how Bernie was doing. Bernie talked about his daughter graduating high school and planning to attend San Francisco State University in the fall. Bernie mentioned that his daughter wanted to be a kindergarten teacher and was busy completing forms to obtain financial aid for college. Bernie talked about being extremely proud of his daughter.

Draven congratulated Bernie and said that he raised a great daughter who would be a wonderful teacher. They even talked about Draven becoming closer to Asia Francisco and her possibly being his girlfriend. He said that he was working on it and hinted that this could be happening soon.

CHAPTER 38

Detective Overstreet called an Uber after leaving the bar and had it drop him off home. He was extremely inebriated and barely made it to the door of his apartment. The room was spinning, and his head hurt. His stomach was nauseated, and he thought about vomiting. He almost passed out, but his dog approached him and started jumping up and down. His tail was wagging, and Little Jimmi looked happy to see his owner. He wondered why his dog was home alone and not next door with the dogsitter.

While engaging in deep thought about this, Jimmi approached Draven, and Draven saw that Jimmi had a note pinned to his collar. He removed the note from Jimmi's collar and read it. It talked about the neighbor dropping Jimmi off at Draven's apartment because she had to take care of a family emergency. Draven wondered why the neighbor did not take him with her to the family emergency. But upon reading the note further, he discovered that she had to go to San Francisco General Hospital, which did not allow dogs in it.

After reading the note, Draven fed Little Jimmi. He looked at Little Jimmi and was amazed at how fast he was growing. He could remember the first day that he adopted Little Jimmi and became a father. He remembered feeling an immediate love for Little Jimmi and a strong desire to keep him safe from the evils of this world. Little Jimmi was so small and scared. He shook all the time and was incredibly scared of strangers along with the world. He could not walk on a leash until receiving all his shots and was as helpless as a child. He was so unsure of the world and other people while worrying if harm would come to himself. With time, he grew to be a self-confident dog, who was bold and ready to take charge of his life.

CHAPTER 39

Detective Overstreet went to see Asia Francisco to talk about the case. He parked his car and proceeded to walk toward the basement of the building that housed the main branch of the San Francisco Police Department in order to get to the forensics lab. While walking to the lab, he smelled incense and heard the gentle humming pertaining to yoga. Draven could see that this was coming from Asia Francisco's forensics lab.

Draven entered the lab and could see Asia in the middle of doing yoga. He could hear a voice in the background instructing Asia to do different poses such as the downward dog and the resting child. Draven noticed that Asia had a mat on the floor, which allowed her to do the poses without destroying her pants.

Detective Overstreet watched Asia as she did her yoga poses. She seemed so graceful and at peace while doing them. Asia was totally focused on the moment and did not seem to have a care in the world. Draven doubted that Asia knew he was in the room because she was deeply involved in her yoga.

Detective Overstreet heard as the voice in the background stopped talking, and he figured that yoga was done for the day. Draven watched as Asia rolled up her yoga mat and put it away and saw her do the same with the CD she was using for yoga. Asia turned around and jumped when she saw Draven in the room. She asked him, "How long have you been standing there?"

He replied, "Long enough."

She then asked him, "What brings you to this dungeon?"

And he replied, "The new body that was brought in for examination."

Draven could feel the tension in the room, but he decided that this was not the time to address it. He had a serial killer on the loose, and the bodies were beginning to pile up. Draven did not have a lead as to the identity of the serial killer, and the city was in the grip of fear because of this madman.

CHAPTER 40

Detective Overstreet asked Asia Francisco if she could tell him anything about the body. Asia said that she appeared to be a Caucasian female in her mid-twenties and had the same puncture marks in her arms and legs as the previous bodies. She informed Draven that there were bruises on the bottom part of both legs and top part of both arms. This was consistent with the other bodies. Asia told Draven that there was no sign of sexual assault and that the victim had a tattoo of a spider on her left arm.

Detective Overstreet asked, "Has the victim been identified yet?"

Asia told him, "So far, she is a Jane Doe. Check upstairs with missing persons to see if anyone had been reported missing recently that matches the description of this victim."

Draven thanked Asia for her assistance and went upstairs to talk to missing persons. He spoke to the officer who was at the scene first when the body had been discovered on the beach. Draven listened as Officer Garcia talked about speaking to a couple who had found the body washed ashore on the beach while playing with their dog. He informed Detective Overstreet that the body was found naked and had not been identified as of yet.

While talking to Officer Garcia, a woman ran frantically into the police station, screaming. "Where is my baby! She never stays out this late without calling me."

Draven saw that the woman was upset and he took her off to the side to speak with her. He asked, "Please describe your daughter."

"She's in her mid-twenties, brown hair, and had a tattoo of a spider on her left arm. She recently obtained employment at Mo Greens."

Detective Overstreet had that look on his face as the woman described her daughter. This individual matched the description of the Jane Doe in the morgue. He said, "We have a Jane Doe that matches the description you provided, and we need assistance identifying it." He took the woman downstairs to the morgue so she could complete the painful process of identifying the body that was once her baby girl. She trembled as Draven escorted her to the morgue and feared the worst.

Once they reached the coroner's office, Detective Overstreet instructed the coroner to lift the sheet covering the body. The women screamed in abject, unrelenting horror. "No, no, no! Not my baby, not my beautiful Roxie!"

Detective Overstreet's heart sank as he watched this. He could feel the woman's pain because her world had just ended. He could see that she would never come back and her heart was permanently broken. He made it his mission to catch this monster and listened as the mother gave him the full name of her daughter. Her name was Roxie Garcia. The mother demanded that he catch this son of a bitch of a killer and make him suffer a hell never experienced by modern man. Draven said, "It would be my pleasure," and he gave her a hug.

CHAPTER 41

Detective Overstreet went to speak with the owner of Mo Greens regarding his impressions of the recently deceased. Mo Greens was located in Market Street in San Francisco, and Draven found parking in the back lot. The first impression that Draven got was that the parking lot was in an isolated location where a person could not be heard if something went wrong. He also noticed that drug usage, homelessness, and mental illness were prevalent in the area.

Detective Overstreet went inside and introduced himself and flashed his detective badge to the worker scanning customer's identification cards before they went into the establishment. She was startled when this happened, but Draven assured her that he was there to talk to the owner about the recent murder of her coworker. The worker left the front desk and went to get the owner.

While waiting to speak to the owner, Draven looked around. He could hear music in the background and recognized it instantly as Cypress Hill's "Insane in the Brain." Draven saw that Mo Greens had three different areas in the store. The first was a lobby with the world's most comfortable couch, the second consisted of the sales floor where all the marijuana and paraphernalia were sold, and the third consisted of a lounge where customers could use their recently purchased marijuana in a safe along with a relaxing environment. The only catch was that if a customer wanted to use the lounge for marijuana, it had to be purchased at this establishment. After looking around, Draven decided that he would come back to this shop later today.

The owner of Mo Greens came to speak to Detective Overstreet. Before doing this, Draven flashed his badge and introduced himself. She in turn introduced herself as D-Rock.

Draven asked D-Rock about her impression of Roxie Garcia. He could tell that she was upset by her murder, so Draven gave her time to answer. D-Rock talked about Roxie recently starting work at Mo Greens. She said that she was a great salesperson who had a sparkling personality that staff and customers liked. D-Rock said she was excited about her upcoming trip to Paris and was busy taking care of several tasks that needed to be completed before the trip.

Draven noticed that this was the second time that one of the victims was going on a trip and needed to take care of some last-minute business before it could take place. When Draven questioned D-Rock further about this, he discovered that these requirements included a replacement California identification and Social Security cards. Draven thanked D-Rock for her assistance and gave her his business card.

CHAPTER 42

Detective Overstreet decided to relay this information to his captain at the police department. Captain Axl Hammer was a no-nonsense individual who did not suffer fools kindly and gave Draven a lot of leeway because of his high clearance rate. Draven thought it was best to update the captain about the case because the captain trusted him completely and he knew, somehow, the case would be solved.

Detective Overstreet pulled his car into the parking lot for the main branch of the police department in San Francisco. Draven was shocked that he was able to find a parking spot this close to the building due to it being late in the morning. After parking his car, Draven proceeded to the captain's office to present him with a status report pertaining to the case that he was investigating.

Draven approached the captain's office and knocked on the door. Captain Hammer told Draven to come in and have a seat. Draven proceeded to give the captain an update about the case. He informed Captain Hammer that he spoke to many individuals regarding the victims in the case and still did not have any leads as to the identity of the killer.

Detective Overstreet said two of the victims were going on vacation soon. He said they were in the process of gathering documents such as California identification and Social Security cards for it. Draven said he was going to follow up on this with the Department of Motor Vehicles and Social Security Administration tomorrow morning. Captain Hammer thanked Draven for the update and Draven said, "You're welcome." Draven proceeded to leave the room.

Before leaving the captain's office, Captain Hammer asked Draven to share a drink with him. He said that his daughter recently completed the requirements to obtain a PhD from the University of San Francisco in psychology and so he wanted to toast her accomplishment. It had been such a harrowing, difficult, downright impossible experience at times, and the captain was proud that his daughter was able to accomplish this task.

CHAPTER 43

Detective Overstreet left Captain Hammer's Office and decided that he wanted to have a drink at EZ5 to unwind. It had been a long but productive day. He got a lot done today and thought that he needed to give himself a reward for his hard work.

He drove himself to EZ5 and parked his car. Draven entered the bar and noticed that one of his closest friends, Bernie Shwartz, was working today. Detective Overstreet ordered his favorite but also standby beer, Grolsch and selected a song on the jukebox. He put his quarter in it and listened to "Patience" by Guns N Roses.

Draven sat down, and he saw someone walk in the door. It was Asia Francisco, and she figured that Draven would be there. She knew that this was his favorite watering hole and he came there regularly to unwind. He began speaking to Asia Francisco about how much he missed her and could not stop thinking about her. She confessed to feeling the same way, and they could see deep within their hearts that they wanted to be much more than friends. With that, they looked deep inside their souls and decided to consummate their love for one another.

Asia got into Draven's car, and they went to her house. They arrived at her house in thirty minutes. The incense went on, and so did the slow music. They settled on "November Rain" by Guns N Roses and went at it like lions on a hot, summer night. She tore off his T-shirt, and he ripped off her skirt. He grabbed her backside and shoved his steel cannon into the forbidden zone. He was halfway to paradise when he could feel the passion rising further. She started howling like a banshee as he did the pelvic thrust with his love wand into the bush. The sweat was pouring out of them, and he could feel a discharge coming as he shoved his face into Asia's bouncing fun bags. It finally happened, and Draven could feel the mother of discharged releases like a dam breaking while his whole body convulsed and then relaxed. He finally reached paradise and had a cigarette to celebrate this accomplishment—nirvana at last.

CHAPTER 44

The night before was a total blur, and so when Draven and Asia woke up the following day, the only thing that they could remember was the sex. They marveled at the copious amounts of empty beer bottles on the floor along with residue that hung in the air from all the incense burned the night before. They were both astonished by all the clothes thrown on the floor when they made passionate love to one another.

Draven made breakfast for Asia. It consisted of eggs, bacon, and waffles with hot chocolate. After that, Asia gave Draven a kiss and thanked him for an unforgettable night. He said, "You're welcome," and began to get ready for work. Before showering, he got in his car and pulled out the extra clothing he kept for special occasions.

Detective Overstreet completed showering and put his clothes on. When done, Draven kissed Asia and said that he would see her later today. With that, he left Asia's house and proceeded to drive himself to work.

CHAPTER 45

Detective Overstreet went home to check on Little Jimmi. He left Little Jimmi with his neighbor before going to work. When Draven went to pick up Little Jimmi from his neighbor's apartment, Little Jimmi started jumping up and down. His tail was wagging, and he was genuinely happy to see him. They were the best of friends and loved each other deeply.

After picking up Little Jimmi from his neighbor's apartment, Draven decided to take him on a walk. He thought about where to go for a moment and decided to take Little Jimmi to Delores Park. It was close to his apartment, and Delores Park was dog-friendly. He could take Little Jimmi off his leash there and allow him to run around without experiencing problems due to reactions from other people.

When Draven arrived at the park, he noticed how lush it was. It was Indian summer, and flowers were beginning to bloom. The air was crisp, and not a breeze was in sight. The grass was moist without it being too wet. The moon was out, and one had a great view of the stars, for there were many in the sky.

They stayed at the park for several hours before deciding to go home. Draven discovered long ago that Little Jimmi slept peacefully after playing and exercising. When they got home, Little Jimmi passed out and slept like an angel free of life's concerns. Draven often noticed that Little Jimmi looked cute and adorable when sleeping.

CHAPTER 46

It was another day at the office. His supervisor was in a mood, and he often equated it to her not having a sex life. She was constantly yelling at people and never in a good mood. The supervisor gave the impression that her supervisees were idiots and incapable of doing their jobs. She constantly micromanaged her staff, and the result was a hatred of her by them.

The killer thought it was time to select another victim. It was almost time, and he thought to himself, *Who would be the next unlucky person?* Suddenly, a smile flashed across his face, and the choice had been made. She was perfect and had everything that he would need from one person. *Tonight was the night,* he thought to himself.

CHAPTER 47

Alyssa McKenzie awoke refreshed and energetic early in the morning. She had a great rest and was ready to begin the day The sun was out and the air crisp. Alyssa put her bikini on and proceeded to get ready for a day at the beach. She selected a hat, suntan oil, and the new book that she recently started reading. It was the newest James Patterson novel, and she was eager to finish it as to ascertain the identity of the killer.

Alyssa was almost ready for her day at the beach. She grabbed the last of her belongings and headed for her car. It was located in the parking lot next to her apartment. Alyssa knew about the recent kidnappings and had her key out so she could get in the car quickly when going to it. She scanned her environment to make sure no one snuck around and tried to grab her.

Alyssa placed her key in the doorknob of the car and heard a noise. She turned around and someone grabbed her. The killer placed a handkerchief around her neck, and she instantly passed out. It was over quickly, and he placed her limp body in his car, which was located nearby. Nobody heard anything, and it was over in an instant.

CHAPTER 48

Alyssa awoke from her slumber, and she noticed that the room was dark. She could barely see a figure in the background, and she said, "What do you want from me?" He did not offer a response and continued to work, ignoring her every word. She just looked around, hoping that the madness would stop and the killer would come to his senses and let her go.

The killer turned on the lights, and the room lit up. She could see pipes and other electrical equipment in the background. A low murmur filled the room, and Alyssa noticed that she was practically naked, except for her bikini. Next to her, lay a table with fentanyl and a syringe. Alyssa started to become nervous and began to scream. She did not know what the killer was going to do and started to repeat the same request over and over again. "Please let me go. No one will ever find out, and I will not say a thing."

All the killer said was, "All will be over soon."

The killer started to prepare the fentanyl. When done, he injected her with the fentanyl, and she quickly fell asleep. He inserted the tubing into her lower legs and upper arms and retrieved the remote control. He did the same with his upper arms and lower legs. The killer hit the red button on the remote control, and the blood transfusion machine started. This process took several hours, and then the transfusion was complete. When done, he wrapped the body in plastic and drove to Baker Beach to drop it off.

CHAPTER 49

Detective Overstreet grabbed the morning paper and proceeded to eat breakfast. He looked at the headlines, and it talked about the heatwave plaguing San Francisco. It mentioned that the temperature would be 90 degrees with 70 percent humidity. Draven thought that this was normal for San Francisco in October and often felt summer vacation should begin in September and last until the end of November in the Bay Area. This was when it was hottest in San Francisco and other neighboring cities. While eating, he received a call from Officer Garcia, who said, "We have another body." Officer Garcia informed Draven that this one was found at Baker Beach too.

He left Little Jimmi to his neighbor and went to the crime scene. The traffic was light, so he was able to make it to the crime scene in twenty minutes. He parked his car and noticed that Asia Francisco was already on the scene. He noticed that she was directing other crime scene technicians to begin the process of dusting the body for prints, taking soil samples, and checking the crime scene for additional evidence. He also watched as Asia shooed onlookers away from the crime scene and reminded police officers that this was a task that they should be performing.

Draven approached Asia and requested information pertaining to the identity of the victim. Draven listened as Asia talked about not being able to identify the victim but said she had small puncture marks on both the bottom of her legs along with top part of the arms. Asia went on to say that there was no sign of a struggle, which included bruising, and mentioned that her skin was chalk white because of total blood drainage from her body. Asia informed Draven that the victim was a female in her mid-twenties and the body had not begun the process of decomposition and was found wrapped in plastic totally naked.

She was able to ascertain that the body was dropped off early in the morning at Baker Beach.

Detective Overstreet requested information pertaining to the identification of the individual who discovered the body. Asia directed him to Officer Garcia who had more information about it. Draven thanked Asia for her assistance, and he went to speak to Officer Garcia about this. He approached Officer Garcia, and he directed him to a teenage girl along with her boyfriend.

Detective Overstreet thanked Officer Garcia for his assistance and went on to speak to the teenager and her boyfriend about this. They talked about playing at the beach and the body washing ashore when engaging in this activity. One of the teenagers mentioned that the body was wrapped in plastic and appeared to be totally naked underneath it. The other teen said she did not touch the body upon discovery and talked about phoning the police right away. Draven thanked the couple for their assistance and gave them his business card.

CHAPTER 50

Detective Overstreet left the crime scene and went to the Department of Motor Vehicles. He arrived at DMV in forty minutes due to the heavy traffic and noted the layout of the building. It was a gray, industrial building surrounded by an expansive parking lot and chained link fence. It did not have any vegetation around it and gave the impression of a building that had seen better days. The paint was chipping, and the exterior had a gray façade that lost its luster long ago.

Draven approached the supervisor and flashed his badge at him. The supervisor was startled and asked for the reason behind his visit. Detective Overstreet told him that there was a serial killer on the loose in San Francisco and he had reason to believe that this person was somehow connected to the Department of Motor Vehicles. Detective Overstreet gave the supervisor the names of two victims who had recently applied for a replacement California identification card, and he asked that he be given the name of the individual who processed them.

The supervisor complied with the request and directed Draven to an electronic database containing this information, and he began his search using it. He quickly found the archived applications and looked for the names and processors. He saw that each of them had a different processor. Draven requested to talk to each of these individuals and was informed that they were not in today. Draven listened as the supervisor said that they would be in tomorrow, so he made an appointment to come back tomorrow morning. He thanked the supervisor for his cooperation and proceeded to exit DMV.

CHAPTER 51

Draven headed back to the squad house and decided to work on completing case reports. He had several case reports to complete, and they were piling up on his desk. Draven wanted to get to them before the paperwork got out of control. He did not want it to reach the point where the paperwork overtook his desk and the desk could not be seen anymore. This happened to another detective in his department before, who was then placed on probation by the captain.

Detective Overstreet focused on the paperwork and was able to complete it in three hours. After that, his mind was fried, so he decided to go home. On the way home, he went to see Asia, and after their conversation, Asia decided to go to Draven's house for dinner and a movie. They went to Vees and ordered hamburgers and fries to go. They settled on watching *The Crow* while eating their food at Draven's house.

They both enjoyed the movie. They loved the atmosphere of the movie and its underlying plot, which consisted of a lover's search for vengeance pertaining to the unsolved murder of his bride. They talked about Brandon Lee being accidentally killed during the filming of it and noted his death as a tragic loss in the world of cinema. They also both agreed that the first *Crow* film was the best one in the franchise and felt that the other entries could not compare to it.

When the movie was over, they talked well into the night. They talked about their experiences in high school, and Draven was shocked to discover that Asia used to be a cheerleader and a blonde. He listened as Asia talked about being unimpressed with that lifestyle and deciding to make a change at that time. Asia informed Draven that she did not have any tattoos along with piercings at this time but changed her appearance after high school, which led to her feeling free and liberated overall.

This conversation continued into dawn. Asia talked about her being popular in high school and getting tired of going to an institution that was overly concerned with physical appearances. She also talked about losing all her friends when she changed her appearance and growing up in a conservative, Italian, Catholic family who were not happy with this.

Draven said, "That must have been hard."

She responded by saying, "Yes, it was, but I got to know who my friends really were."

He listened as she talked about moving out of her house after graduating high school and deciding to attend the forensics program at San Francisco State University and graduating with honors.

They were both exhausted, so Draven decided to carry Asia to his bed. She could barely walk and was out on her feet. He placed Asia in his bed, and Little Jimmi jumped in. Little Jimmi slept next to Asia and had grown to love her immediately to the point that Little Jimmi wanted to protect her from outside harm. Draven noted this and thought to himself, *She must have a warm heart because Little Jimmi has never been like this to someone before. It happened immediately.* He crawled into bed, and all three were in complete bliss, secure with one another and free of all worldly worries.

CHAPTER 52

Draven awoke the following morning, and Asia was still asleep. She was curled up in a ball with her long, black hair covering her backside. He could see a huge tattoo on her back but could not ascertain the design of it. Asia's shirt was covering it. He saw Asia holding Little Jimmi, and they looked so peaceful. They looked as if they were completely serene and did not have a care in the world.

He then went to the store to pick out a bouquet of roses. He picked out a card and wrote a beautiful note for Asia thanking her for a wonderful and magical night. He then selected a carton of eggs, bacon, and coffee. He decided that he was going to make breakfast in bed for Asia to show his deep love for her.

Draven paid for these items and drove back to his apartment. He made breakfast for Asia and left one of the roses along with a note on the pillow next to her. The rest were placed in a vase in the living room. He wanted it to be the first thing she sees when she wakes up. Draven just needed to make sure that he was not to loud while doing this.

He proceeded to make breakfast for Asia, consisting of eggs, bacon, and hash browns along with coffee. Asia awoke, and the first thing she noticed was the smell coming from the kitchen. She saw the rose and the note attached to it. She read it, and it made her smile. Deep inside, she could hear herself saying, "I love this man, and I am ready to spend my life with him forever." With that, she went downstairs and hugged him while whispering, "I love you, and it is forever," in his ear. Little Jimmi was jumping up and down while this was happening and could tell his pack had a permanent family member whom he loved.

CHAPTER 53

Detective Overstreet left his apartment and proceeded to the Department of Motor Vehicles. He thought about the magical night he had with Asia and could not believe that she was officially his girlfriend. He thought about Little Jimmi deciding to cuddle up with Asia in his bed, and looking back, he saw that his dog was guiding him toward the right decision. He was so happy inside and finally was able to secure a lifelong dream: Asia as his girlfriend. She was the girl of his dreams, and he began to see that the more he got to know her.

Draven pulled into the parking lot. He parked his car and proceeded to enter the building. Draven approached the supervisor, whom he spoke to yesterday, and was immediately directed to a conference room where a worker from DMV was sitting behind a desk. He looked scared and nervous. His legs were shaking, and sweat was pouring down his face. Draven thought to himself, *He probably does not know what is going to happen, and this is making him nervous.*

Detective Overstreet flashed his badge to the worker and introduced himself. He informed the worker that he had a few questions about Lisa Miranda's application for a replacement California identification card. Before proceeding any further, Detective Overstreet asked the worker for his name. He responded by saying, "Herman Garcia."

Draven then went on to ask, "Regarding Lisa Miranda, what could you tell me about her application for a replacement California identification card?"

Mr. Garcia said, "Lisa needed it for an upcoming trip to Paris, which she confessed to being excited about. I admit I was attracted to her and wanted to get to know Lisa further, but I was scared to do this."

Draven felt that this man had nothing to do with the murder and did not give off an aura of a killer but seemed more like a sexually repressed male trapped inside an adult's body. He just seemed too awkward, while the killer was calm, cool, organized, and confident in his demeanor. But Draven decided a polygraph test would be needed to rule out any further doubts. With that, Draven thanked Mr. Garcia for his assistance and told him that a polygraph test would take place tomorrow morning. He gave Mr. Garcia the address of the police station where the polygraph test would take place and proceeded to get the second worker waiting outside the conference room.

Detective Overstreet followed the same format with the second worker. The only difference was that this line of questioning pertained to an application for a replacement California identification card for Trish Armstrong. She had an upcoming trip to Paris like the previous victim. The second worker identified himself as Ryan Thompson. He did not fit the mold of a serial killer either. Draven also ordered a polygraph test for this individual to rule out any doubts.

Detective Overstreet thanked the supervisor for his assistance and left the department. He thought that the morning was a total bust and waste of time. Neither of the two workers fit the mold of a serial killer. Draven thought to himself, *I am no closer to catching the killer since first being assigned the case. I still do not have a break as to the identity of the killer, and time is running out.* Draven could tell that he was starting to get frustrated with the lack of progress in his case and decided to go to the gym to relieve some stress.

CHAPTER 54

Draven arrived at the gym. He was eager to begin his workout and start the process of stress reduction. Draven started his workout with a twenty-minute bike ride and then proceeded to do crunches along with chin-ups. He could feel the stress peeling away from his body as he progressed through each exercise. It was something that he knew he needed.

Detective Overstreet then began working on his deltoids and other muscles. He went slow to make sure that he got the form of the exercise correct. He was taught to go slow and pay attention to the impact it had on the different parts of his body. If he felt pain or soreness in one part that the exercise was not intended to work out, then he was doing it wrong.

Draven worked out for an hour and a half. He showered and then took Asia out to dinner at Joe's of Westlake. Joe's of Westlake was an institution in the area, and it was the go-to restaurant. They had great food with generous portions. It was common knowledge that most people could not complete eating their meal because the portions were big. They ended up taking the rest home and having it for lunch the following day.

CHAPTER 55

Draven was excited because the weekend came and he would get to spend it with his two favorite people: his dog and girlfriend. He decided that they were going to the beach because it was a beautiful, sunny day. It was a shame to spend it indoors. The air was crisp, and not a cloud was in the sky. There was a slight breeze in the air, and the hummingbirds were singing as if begging everyone to go outside.

They packed into Draven's car and prepared to go to the beach. Before going, Draven made sure to bring his glasses and suntan oil. He retrieved these items along with Little Jimmi's leash and then proceeded to drive them to the beach. They stopped off at Safeway before going to the beach and picked up a six pack of Lagunitas beer. It was one of Draven's favorites, and it turned out that Asia liked it too.

They arrived at the beach and parked the car. Little Jimmi was excited to go to the beach and was jumping up and down. He was eager to let the ice-cold water envelope his fur. As they approached the beach and started walking on the sand, Little Jimmi was jumping out of his harness and wanted to let loose on the water. Draven undid the harness, and Little Jimmi was loose. He ran and ran until finally passing out from exhaustion.

In the meantime, Asia set up a small barbeque pit and took off her skirt. She had various tattoos along her arms and legs plus piercings. Draven was watching as everyone stared at Asia in total disbelief, and he could only think, *Eat your hearts out, she is all mine*. Asia prepared the barbeque pit and, when done, brought the premade hamburgers out. She made three of them and corn on the cob with potato salad. While waiting for the food, they listened to various songs in anticipation of the feast that awaited them. The food was finally ready, and they devoured it. It was delicious, and besides being a ravenous beauty, Asia was a great cook, who made everything with such care and precision to detail.

They were at the beach well into the night. They decided to stay and watch the sun go down. Draven brought a bottle of red wine and poured a glass for him and Asia. They watched the sun go down together, and after that, Draven professed his undying love for Asia. They did the deed and, once again, sealed the deal. Little Jimmi was passed out and heard nothing.

CHAPTER 56

Detective Overstreet could feel that the case was starting to get to him. He felt the tension boiling in his stomach and noticed increasing difficulties with falling asleep. Draven began eating less and noticed that he was becoming more impatient with Asia and, sometimes, Little Jimmi. He did not like the person that he was becoming and decided that consulting another individual about the case would be helpful. With that, he decided to consult his trusted and loyal friend, Pit Bull Feliciano, the next day. After that, he felt the tension leave his body and quickly fell asleep.

Draven drove to Pit Bull's house early in the morning. Pit Bull lived in a huge mansion with his dog, Sobriety. Sobriety was a pit bull, similar to Little Jimmi, and they frequently played together. The house was located in the Sea Cliff District of San Francisco and had its own swimming pool along with a basketball court. The house was surrounded by a fence where a guard buzzed visitors in. Pit Bull had his own private security company and had made a fortune in it. *Not bad for someone who had a rough start in life,* Draven thought to himself.

Draven arrived at the house, and the guard buzzed him in. He hugged Pit Bull and thanked him for agreeing to be of assistance in this case. Pit Bull was an Italian male in his forties, who used to be a Marine sniper and was known to be a stallion in bed. He had muscle tone and followed a strict diet of exercise to maintain his physique. His only vice was marijuana, which helped him in more ways than one.

They sat down on a table in the patio, and Draven noticed that the chessboard was out. They agreed that after talking about the case and ascertaining the next course of action to take to solve it, a chess game was in order. Draven laid out the details of the case for Pit Bull, and Pit Bull listened with rapt attention. Pit

Bull had a real nose for details because of his military training and other experiences, which Draven thought could be really helpful in solving the case. When Draven was done talking, Pit Bull reminded him that the killer was a smart, plodding man and the only way to ascertain his identity is to pay attention to the details of the case. The details would give away his identity soon enough. The last bit of advice that Pit Bull could offer Draven regarding the case was to follow up with that lead at the Social Security Administration and be aware of the pattern. All killers had a pattern and method of operation. Draven just had to identify and discover it.

After this, they played a game of chess before Draven had to go back to the squad house. He had paperwork to complete pertaining to the case and did not want his desk to become overwhelmed with it. The chess game lasted for forty-five minutes, and Draven lost in the end. It did not bother Draven because he liked the strategy of the game and enjoyed his discussions with Pit Bull. Plus, he enjoyed the battle of wits.

CHAPTER 57

Draven headed back to the squad house and started working on his paperwork. He thought to himself, *How is the killer selecting his victims? There has to be a pattern.* His thoughts were interrupted by the loud musings of Captain Hammer. He could tell that Captain Hammer was on the telephone and the person on the other end was yelling at him. He could tell that this person was an authority figure and guessed that it was probably the mayor. When the conversation was over, Draven heard the captain slam down the phone and almost throw it against the wall.

Detective Overstreet approached Captain Hammer and felt that he needed to talk to him. They had been friends for a long time, and Draven could tell that the conversation upset Captain Hammer deeply. When walking into the captain's office, Draven noticed that the captain had poured himself a glass of Johnny Walker Red Label and offered Draven one. Draven accepted, and they talked about the pressure that the mayor's office was placing on the police department to discover the identity of the killer. Captain Hammer talked about having every officer work on the case around the clock and they still could not ascertain the identity of the killer.

While speaking to the captain, Draven noticed that Captain Hammer was calming down and feeling less angry about the telephone call with the mayor. Both thought that this could probably be due to intoxication, and they laughed about it. Before they knew it, the whole bottle was empty. At least, the captain was calm and not so angry about the telephone conversation with the mayor.

CHAPTER 58

Draven awoke and got ready for work. He showered and put on his black jeans and Rob Zombie T-shirt. Draven put on his black-and- white Converse tennis shoes and selected the rings that he wanted to wear that day and put them on his fingers. He did the same with his Svengoolie watch cap, sunglasses, and skull scarf. Draven retrieved Little Jimmi and left him with his neighbor, who usually watched Little Jimmi when he went to work.

Little Jimmi was exceptionally playful, and it took him a while to calm down. He was a happy dog who always woke up cheerful each morning, ready to greet Draven. Today, Little Jimmi wanted Draven to stay home and spend the day with him. Draven could tell that Little Jimmi was upset about him having to go to work, but as the morning progressed, he came to understand that he had to do this in order to pay the bills.

Draven planned to speak to the supervisor of the Social Security Administration. He wanted to speak to this individual about seeking permission to talk to the caseworker who processed Lisa Miranda and Trish Armstrong's applications for a replacement Social Security card. He remembered what Pit Bull said earlier in the week about paying attention to details and thought that a clue as to the identity of the killer, possibly, lie in these victims' applications. Draven wanted to pursue every possible lead in order to discover the identity of the serial killer.

He drove to the Social Security Administration on Kearney Street. On the way over, he stopped at the All-Star Café and had a donut along with herbal tea. He found that herbal tea assisted him in calming down his nerves and anxiety, and this case was testing them. After eating, he came back to his car and continued on his journey.

Draven noticed that traffic was exceptionally bad that day. It was bumper to bumper, and going to the Social Security Administration took longer than usual. He finally arrived at his destination and was able to find a parking space, which also took a while. He then paid the meter and proceeded to walk inside the building.

Detective Overstreet felt the sun on his back as he walked to the Social Security Administration. The air was crisp, and Draven could feel a breeze in the air. The hummingbirds were singing, and the streets were simmering with people. It felt as if everyone knew today would be a beautiful day and they wanted to take advantage of it.

Draven reached the Social Security Administration office and entered it. He flashed his badge to the security guard and introduced himself as Detective Overstreet from the San Francisco Police Department. He went on to say that he needed to speak to the supervisor about this individual being of assistance pertaining to an ongoing police investigation. The security guard escorted Detective Overstreet into the administrative section of the building and led him into the office of Walter Sampson, the supervisor of the Social Security Administration, as indicated on the nameplate.

Detective Overstreet introduced himself to Walter Sampson and flashed his badge. Walter asked, "What is this about?"

Detective Overstreet said, "I would like to ask if you could be of assistance in an ongoing police investigation pertaining to the murders of young women in San Francisco. We have reason to believe that the suspect might be working in this office and would like to speak to the individual who processed the applications of two of the victims who requested a replacement Social Security card."

The supervisor said, "This information is archived and placed in a database located in the basement of this building."

Draven requested access to it, and the supervisor agreed to let him have it. Then Mr. Sampson's administrative assistant, Leslie James, approached him and said, "Follow me." She proceeded to lead him to the database that housed the information he requested. Draven followed her to a room in the basement. They stopped at a door, and Leslie pulled out a card for scanning so they could enter the room. She did this, and the door opened. Upon entering the room, he saw a giant supercomputer. Miss James placed her login information into the computer and, when done, informed Draven that it was ready for usage.

Detective Overstreet typed Lisa Miranda and Trish Armstrong's names in the computer. He was then directed to another screen that stated the purpose of request. He highlighted *Social Security Card Applications* and hit *search*. A name flashed on the screen, and a paper was instantly printed out for Draven. It said Oscar Mattingly. He wondered if this could be the lead that he was searching for all these months. *Do I finally have this animal nailed to the wall?* Draven thought so and was so excited to have a strong lead as to the identity of the killer. He wanted to detain this individual and begin questioning him.

Detective Overstreet logged out of the computer and went to talk to Mr. Sampson about his recent discovery. He approached the supervisor and informed him that he needed to speak to Oscar Mattingly. Draven told Mr. Sampson, "We are looking into Oscar Mattingly in the murder of Lisa Miranda and Trish Sampson and possibly several other women."

Mr. Sampson said, "This could not be true because Oscar is a family man and does not seem like the sort of person who could perform these heinous acts."

Draven again informed the supervisor that he needed to speak to Oscar Mattingly. Mr. Sampson escorted Draven to Oscar Mattingly's cubicle and watched as Detective Overstreet read the suspect his Miranda Rights. He then placed handcuffs on Oscar and informed him that he was under arrest for the murder of Lisa Miranda and Trish Armstrong.

Oscar said, "I did not do this, and I demand to speak to a lawyer." Mr. Sampson could not believe what was happening and watched as Draven arrested Oscar and placed him in his car in order to be transferred to the squad office for further questioning.

CHAPTER 59

Draven arrived at the police station with Oscar Mattingly. He gave the suspect to the officer on duty, and Mr. Mattingly was immediately placed in a holding cell. While doing this, Detective Overstreet could hear Captain Hammer screaming. He said, "Has Draven lost his mind, and is he trying to give me a heart attack? We do not transport suspects to the police station in our own cars and arrest them without having more evidence." Draven then decided that he better let the captain calm down before giving him an update on the case.

In the background, Draven could hear a man identifying himself as Taylor Wilmingham, ESQ demanding to speak to Oscar Mattingly. Detective Overstreet then heard the officer on duty inform Mr. Wilmingham that Oscar was in a holding cell waiting to speak to Detective Overstreet. He then heard Mr. Wilmingham demand to speak to Captain Hammer about the unlawful detention of Mr. Mattingly and urge him to be released immediately. The officer on duty directed him to Captain Hammer's office and knew that the show would soon begin.

CHAPTER 60

Detective Overstreet waited until the captain calmed down before going into his office. It took an hour before this happened, and even so, he still approached him with caution. He entered the captain's office and saw him visibly upset but able to regain some self-control.

"I hope you know what you're doing because I'm taking a lot of flak about the arrest of Oscar Mattingly from the mayor's office."

Draven said to the captain, "Even if I have the wrong suspect, I still feel that we are on the right path because the killer works in that building. I could feel it in my gut."

Captain Hammer then said, "I know and trust you are doing the right thing." He then informed Draven that Oscar's lawyer was in the building, demanding that his client be released due to wrongful detainment and imprisonment.

Detective Overstreet said, "I know and saw this person speaking to the officer on duty earlier today."

Captain Hammer then said, "Oscar's lawyer was right, and we could only hold him for three hours. He could be released after that if he was not charged with a crime." Then he added, "You have three hours to find something that we could charge him with. Otherwise, we have to let him go."

With that, Draven left Captain Hammer's office and went to talk to the suspect.

CHAPTER 61

Draven had Officer Garcia escort Oscar Mattingly to the conference room where he was at. The conference room was small and faintly lit. The air conditioner was on, and a table along with two chairs stood in the middle of it. They both faced a one-way mirror where other detectives and police personal could watch, from another room, as Draven spoke to the suspect. A door stood on the left side so police personnel could enter and leave the room.

Oscar Mattingly entered the room and sat down. He looked scared and had problems making eye contact with Detective Overstreet. Draven asked Oscar, "Do you want something to drink to decrease the underlying tension in the room?"

Oscar said, "Yes," and Draven presented him with a glass of water. Draven then brought out a tape recorder and informed Oscar that he was going to make a recording of the conversation. After that, Draven asked Oscar for his name, and Oscar obliged.

Draven then proceeded further with questioning. "What is your relationship to the murdered women?" asked Draven.

Oscar said, "I did not have one prior to them entering my office to apply for replacement Social Security cards."

He then asked Oscar, "What were you doing on the nights these women were murdered?"

Oscar talked about being at a party with his girlfriend. Draven then asked for her name along with contact information so his story could be corroborated and watched as Oscar presented it to him. He also asked for the name of anyone, besides his girlfriend, who could verify his whereabouts on those dates. Draven was given the name of Leonard Washington. Leonard was Oscar's best friend and was at the same parties he was at on the nights in question.

CHAPTER 62

The killer watched with great delight as the situation unfolded around him. He could not believe how incompetent the police were, and a smile flashed across his face as he thought about it. He watched them as they arrested the wrong person and marveled at how fast they were to make an arrest with a slim, almost nonexistent, amount of evidence. He could not believe how recklessly the police operated and thought to himself, *Oscar has a hell of a lawsuit on his hands. They were so quick to violate someone's civil rights.*

The killer loved the cat-and-mouse game that he was playing between himself and the police department. He loved being able to outwit and outthink them at every pass. He was able to think various moves ahead of the police and had them totally frazzled. He thought to himself, *They are grasping at straws and desperate to find a suspect so this case could be closed. So much fun to watch them squirm and fall straight on their faces.* With these thoughts in mind, he went about his business at work and felt a smile flash subconsciously through his mind as he thought about the police bungling through the case.

CHAPTER 63

Draven had Officer Garcia escort the suspect back to the holding cell after he spoke to him in the conference room. He decided that the next course of action would be to talk to Leonard Washington about Oscar's whereabouts on the nights of the murders. Draven had two more hours to hold the suspect for questioning before he was eligible to be released from police custody due to lack of evidence needed to charge him with a crime. And with the lawyer here, Oscar's release was a forgone conclusion.

Detective Overstreet went back to his office and decided to contact Leonard Washington via telephone. He dialed the number, and a male voice answered immediately. The voice identified himself as Leonard Washington, and Draven identified himself as Detective Overstreet from the San Francisco Police Department. The other voice seemed startled and asked, "What is this about?"

Draven said, "I have Oscar Mattingly in police custody, and he is a person of interest pertaining to two unsolved murders."

Leonard said, "I want to be of assistance however I can, and Oscar could never do this. He is a warm, gentle family man."

Draven continued with the conversation, and he talked about wanting to speak to Leonard in person immediately. Leonard said, "We could meet at Starbucks near my office in twenty minutes," and Draven confirmed the appointment. Leonard gave Draven the address of Starbucks, and the call ended. Draven proceeded to go walk to Starbucks on Market Street to speak to Leonard about the whereabouts of Oscar on the night of the two murders.

CHAPTER 64

Detective Overstreet walked to Starbucks on Market Street to meet with Leornard Washington. On his way to the coffee shop, he saw that foot traffic in the neighborhood was light, and so he was at Starbucks in minutes. The building had a huge courtyard surrounding it, and he noticed that there was a lot of people in the courtyard enjoying the nice, beautiful day. Draven lived here all his life and knew that a warm, beautiful day was a luxury that you wanted to take advantage of.

Draven entered Starbucks and went to find a seat. He looked around and did not see anyone matching Leonard's description. Draven decided to order an herbal tea and proceeded to wait for someone matching Leonard's description to enter the building. He waited thirty minutes before someone matching Leonard's description walked into the building.

Detective Overstreet noticed that this individual was wearing a suit. That was different from other patrons at the coffeehouse who were wearing jeans and t-shirts. This individual was of African American descent, and he was wearing a tie with his nicely tailored suit. As part of his suit, he wore a vest and had a college ring on his finger to signal that he graduated from an institution of higher learning. Leonard also wore glasses and was carrying a briefcase.

Detective Overstreet signaled to Leonard with his hands that he was sitting at the back of the coffeehouse. Leonard saw Draven doing this and started to walk toward him. Right away, Draven could see that Leonard was a self-assured man because of the assertive way he walked and carried himself physically. He gave the aura of a man who knew what he wanted and would not give up until it became a reality.

Leonard sat down and introduced himself to Detective Overstreet. Draven, in turn, flashed his badge at Leonard and proceeded to explain to him that Oscar was a person of interest in two unsolved murders. He went on to say, "Oscar is currently in police custody, and when asked about his whereabouts the nights of the murders, he reported being at two separate parties that you could corroborate." Leonard nodded to Draven to signal that he was following and listening to what was said intensely. Detective Overstreet then asked, "Was Oscar at two separate parties the nights of the murders?"

He said, "Yes. My wife was also with us all night at these two parties. She, along with several other people, could verify this."

Draven requested the name of Leonard's wife along with her contact information. He then asked for the names and contact information of several other people at these two parties. Leonard watched as Draven contacted these people via telephone. Draven listened as these people confirmed that Oscar was at these two parties the nights of the murders. Draven thanked them for their assistance and hung up the phone. He then thanked Leonard for his cooperation and assistance and exited the coffeehouse to go back to the squad house. He needed to complete more paperwork and explore the next course of action to take in his attempt to solve the case.

CHAPTER 65

While walking back to the squad house, Draven could feel himself becoming frustrated with the lack of progress in the case. He thought that he finally had a lead as to the identity of the killer and was disappointed that it did not pan out. Draven said, "I still do not have a lead that could point me to the identity of the killer, and the bodies are beginning to pile up." He thought about this during his entire walk back to the squad house and decided that he needed to consult with Captain Hammer pertaining to the next course of action to take.

Draven arrived at the squad house and went to see Captain Hammer. Captain Hammer saw Draven approaching his office and poked his head out the front door. He could tell that something was bothering Draven and told him to come in. Captain Hammer put a chair next to his desk and asked Draven to have a seat. Draven then began to voice his frustration with the case in regard to finding a lead as to the identity of the killer.

Captain Hammer had Draven review the details of the case with him. They went over each part of it meticulously in an attempt to locate any shred of detail that was missed at this point. After doing this, Captain Hammer advised Draven to consult more with Asia Francisco if she had any updates pertaining to the case. He reminded Draven that Asia constantly examined evidence pertaining to ongoing cases and could possibly have a lead. In order to confirm that, Captain Hammer reminded Draven that he needed to consult with Asia on a more frequent and ongoing basis.

CHAPTER 66

Draven headed to the forensics lab where Asia Francisco worked. He arrived at the building and entered it. While walking to the forensics lab, he heard a faint sound coming from the end of the hall, and it became clearer as Draven got closer to the forensics lab. He recognized the sound of "Dear Prudence" by Siouxsie and the Banshees. He peered through the window and noticed that Asia was dancing to the music while completing the last part of analyzing evidence from a case. He thought to himself, *I never knew that she could dance and she could really move. I cannot wait to get her on the dance floor.*

Draven slowly opened the door and quietly entered the lab. He could hear her singing as well as dancing to the music. He thought that she had a nice voice and had never heard her sing before. He thought to himself again, *So much for the myth of the sad Goth.* Detective Overstreet knew that people in the Goth subculture were portrayed as being depressed by the mainstream media because they enjoyed piercings, tattoos, and scary movies and dressed in black. But most Goths Draven knew were happy and very comfortable in their own skin.

The music stopped, and Asia asked Alexa to play "First, Last, and Always" by The Sisters of Mercy. While Alexa was playing that song, Asia went to light some incense in her burner, and she jumped out of her skin when she saw Draven in the room. She asked him, "How long have you been there?"

He replied, "Long enough to hear the voice and see the dance moves that you have been hiding from me."

Asia said, "I have not been hiding them. I just have not had a chance to show them to you."

Draven asked, "How about this weekend at The Death Guild?"

Asia said, "Yes."

Draven replied, "See you at ten."

With all this talk, Draven almost forgot about the reason behind him initially going to see Asia in the forensics lab. The only thing that he knew at that particular moment was that he was physically attracted to Asia and the case was the farthest thing from his mind. With that in mind, he began thinking about the victims of the killer and was able to regain his focus on the case.

Draven asked Asia, "Do you have any updates pertaining to the case?"

"I did discover some fibers under Lisa Miranda's fingernails and found that they were cotton fibers. I analyzed them further, and they matched those normally found on a black sweatshirt."

Draven commented, "The killer must have worn a black sweatshirt when he kidnapped Lisa, and Lisa must have fought back while being abducted." He then asked, "Do you have any additional evidence?"

"The bruise marks I found on the top part of both arms and bottom part of both legs were stress marks from leather straps used to tie them down. I analyzed the puncture wounds, and they matched those used for small tubes that could have been inserted into their skin and used to drain blood."

Draven, seemingly shocked by the news that blood had been drained from all of the victims' bodies, said, "That is the connection. The blood." He then reviewed the details of the case in his mind. *The killer is draining these women's blood using tubes. He is kidnapping them at night and tying the women down using leather straps. The killer must be using a machine to drain blood from their bodies, and that could possibly be at his residence. But who has access to this information to select the victims?* he thought to himself.

CHAPTER 67

The killer sat at home and watched television. He buttered his muffin and watched the morning news on Channel 4. The killer watched as the anchorwoman talked about the unsolved murders that were spreading fear throughout San Francisco, and a smile flashed on his face. The anchorwoman went on to say that Det. Draven Overstreet was handling the case, and he watched as a picture of this individual flashed on the screen. The killer thought, *Now I have someone worthy of the game. Let's play.*

The killer pulled out his scrapbook and began to look it over. It had clippings of articles detailing all the murdered victims that were found throughout San Francisco. The killer started to become aroused while looking it over, and he decided that another clipping needed to be added to the scrapbook. The killer took out today's paper and cut out an article identifying Draven Overstreet as the lead detective handling the case. He then pasted it to the scrapbook. *What a nice addition*, he thought to himself and proceeded to finish his breakfast.

CHAPTER 68

Detective Overstreet headed home to his apartment for the night. It had been a long day, and he was eager to relax with Little Jimmi. Before arriving home, he went to his neighbor's apartment and retrieved Little Jimmi. When his neighbor opened the door, Little Jimmi came out and started licking Draven's cheeks. He started barking, and Draven grabbed Little Jimmi and gave him a kiss. Man and dog were reunited, and it brought an end to a chaotic day.

Draven brought Little Jimmi into the apartment and prepared his dinner. It consisted of homemade rice, carrots, and chicken. Little Jimmi started jumping up and down and seemed to be drooling at the thought of the feast that awaited him. He kept staring at the food and appeared to be eager to devour it.

Draven presented Little Jimmi his dinner and noticed that Little Jimmi seemed wobbly and started having problems standing up. Little Jimmi vomited and started shaking. Draven became scared and grabbed Little Jimmi. He placed his shaky body into a towel and loaded him into the car so he could be transported to Sage Emergency Veterinary Services.

Draven drove like a madman to Sage Emergency Veterinary Services at 201 Alabama Street. He thought that he was going to lose Little Jimmi, and that absolutely horrified him. Draven could feel his heart breaking and thoughts racing but was able to calm down and focus on the task at hand. Draven arrived at Sage Emergency Veterinary Services and calmly brought Little Jimmi to the reception desk. He told the receptionist Little Jimmi's symptoms, and she presented him with paperwork to fill out while waiting to see the veterinarian.

When done, she brought Draven into an examination room with Little Jimmi, and they waited for the veterinarian. She could tell that Draven was scared to death of losing Little Jimmi and on the verge of tears. The receptionist gave Draven a hug and said, "Do not worry. It will be all right, and Little Jimmi is in good hands."

Draven waited for ten minutes before the veterinarian came in, and that seemed like an eternity. He kept imagining the worst and thought that he was going to lose the best friend he ever had. They were the best of friends and had been through everything together. He loved his dog deeply, and nothing could replace him. The thought of burying his best friend destroyed him inside. He could feel that his heart was breaking and shattering.

The veterinarian came in, and she introduced herself as Dr. Sullivan. Draven informed her of Little Jimmi's symptoms, and the veterinarian could tell that Draven was scared to death of losing his dog. After hearing Little Jimmi's symptoms, Dr. Sullivan said, "It could be something that he ate." She took Little Jimmi to another room for an x-ray, came back several minutes later, and said, "The x-ray showed that he was experiencing indigestion from something he ate." She gave Little Jimmi a pill and said, "That should clear his stomach up in several hours." Within minutes, Draven could see that Little Jimmi was back to his old self. She advised Draven to bring Little Jimmi back if the symptoms persist after several days.

Draven felt relieved and hugged Little Jimmi. He pet his fur, which felt like silk, and gave him a kiss. Draven was so happy that it was not serious and took his best friend back to the car. On the way home, he bought Little Jimmi a toy. Later that night, he tucked Little Jimmi in his bed, covered him up, and gave him a kiss. He petted him and thanked Little Jimmi for being his best friend and said, "I love you."

CHAPTER 69

Draven was walking across a long tunnel. It was dark, damp, and cold. He could not see anything around him except total darkness. He reached around and could feel the cold concrete that surrounded him. Draven could hear a woman screaming, and he could not tell what direction it was coming from. He continued to have his hands out in front of him as he was walking in the hope of finding a way out of this.

As he walked along the tunnel, the screams became louder and more pronounced. He still could not identify as to whom the screams were coming from. Suddenly, the lights came on, and he could see the tunnel that he was walking along more clearly. On the floor lay case files of murdered victims, and the covers had blood on them. He tried opening the files but ended up getting blood all over his hands.

Draven heard a loud, piercing scream and saw a figure at the end of the tunnel. He ran toward it and noticed a door opened at the end of the tunnel, where the figure went into. He ran to the door and went in. He was not sure what was on the other side but felt it must have been important. Draven walked in and saw the macabre scene that lay beside him. It was Asia Francisco, and she was dead. She lay naked on the floor and was wrapped in plastic. Her skin was pale, and all her blood had been drained from her body.

Beyond that, he could not see anything else that had been done to the body. When bending over to examine the body in greater detail, he saw a note attached to it that read: "You will never catch me." Then he started to scream and convulse violently, knowing that his life was over. The killer had taken the only person, other than Little Jimmi, who meant everything to him. His heart was completely broken and shattered.

Detective Overstreet awoke, and his heart was racing. Sweat was pouring out of his body, and he could barely speak. His system was in total shock. Little Jimmi came over to Draven and started licking him. Draven thought to himself, *What a nightmare, and it felt so real.* He attempted to go back to sleep, but that proved to be impossible. He took Little Jimmi for a walk, and that seemed to calm him down. After that, Draven went back to his apartment and fell asleep.

CHAPTER 70

The following day, Draven decided that he needed to clear his mind and went to the gym. He decided that he needed to have a day removed from murder and mayhem. Draven needed to do something that would let his mind wander and unwind so he could be able to examine the case more clearly and put it together more proficiently in his mind. He found that in the past, physical exercise could achieve this goal.

Draven parked his car and went to 24-hour Fitness. He had a membership with them since 2020 and loved the fact that they were open twenty-four hours a day. He sometimes needed to work out at night and, on more than one occasion, would exercise after work. This had proven to be extremely relaxing in the past for him.

He started his exercise regimen with a fifteen-minute workout on the bike and then did stomach crunches along with pull-ups. Draven found that pull-ups were one of the most difficult exercises to complete, but that only made him stronger and more agile. Draven then proceeded to work out his deltoids, quads, and other parts of his body with free weights along with the machines. Draven could feel the stress peel off his body as he did each exercise. By the time he was done with his exercises, Draven could feel a sense of relaxation and inner peace taking over his body. He thought, *That is what I have been looking for and it has arrived at last.* Then he took a shower, dressed, and went to get something to eat.

Detective Overstreet drove to Original Joe's in North Beach and ordered spaghetti with meatballs. He made sure to tell the waiter to add sausage and bring sourdough bread as part of the meal. He was starving and salivating at the thought of his upcoming meal. He could smell the spaghetti as the cook made it, and his tastebuds were inflamed with hunger. It finally came, and Draven devoured it in minutes. He was shocked because the portions were huge, and Draven never finished a whole meal before. He usually had to take some of it home as lunch for the following day. Before going, he left a generous tip and ordered spaghetti and meatballs to go for Asia. He planned to drop it off at the forensics lab later on the way home.

CHAPTER 71

Draven dropped off the spaghetti and meatball dinner to Asia. She was starving and thanked Draven for the meal. Asia talked about being swamped with evidence that needed to be processed and analyzed for the other cases, which prevented her from eating breakfast and lunch today. Draven noticed that Asia looked exhausted and gathered that she had been up for twenty-four hours in order to process and analyze all the backlogged evidence for the cases.

Detective Overstreet listened as Asia talked about being exhausted and needing to take a nap. Asia looked like she was going to collapse from sleep deprivation, so Draven suggested, "Go home immediately because it's unhealthy to be up that long without adequate rest."

Asia said, "I am going home after I am done processing and analyzing the evidence, which would be completed soon." Draven kissed Asia on the cheek and said, "I'll talk to you later."

He left the forensics lab and decided to head to Pit Bull Feliciano's residence to talk about the case. He hoped he could give him more advice as to how to identify and catch the killer because Draven was running out of ideas.

CHAPTER 72

Draven drove to Pit Bull Feliciano's residence. Upon arriving, outside, he dialed Pit Bull's telephone number on the dial pad near the front gate and listened as Pit Bull Feliciano answered the phone. Draven informed Pit Bull that he was outside the gate, and Pit Bull buzzed him in. Draven proceeded to enter Pit Bull's residence.

He marveled at the sight of it. He had been here before, but the opulence never ceased to shock and amaze him. He noticed that Pit Bull still had the outdoor basketball court and indoor Olympic-sized swimming pool. Draven saw that Pit Bull had the Ferrari in the driveway along with the recently purchased Lamborghini. He noticed that Pit Bull was in the process of creating a lush outdoor garden and firepit. He also saw that Sobriety had an enclosure with an outdoor doghouse and grassy field where he could play and relieve himself as needed.

Draven and Pit Bull sat down and began discussing the details of the case. Beers were brought by Pit Bull's girlfriend who he introduced to Draven. Draven thanked Pit Bull's girlfriend and began presenting Pit Bull with details pertaining to the progress of the case. Pit Bull listened with rapt attention and saved his advice for when Draven finished talking. When Draven was done speaking, Pit Bull advised him that the key to solving this case entailed ascertaining the blood type of the victims. He informed Draven that this variable was how the victims were being selected by the killer.

He said, "You need to find out who has access to this information because one of those people is the killer. The killer is a chameleon who blends into the background. So look for someone who is quiet and conscientious about their work and does not make waves." Draven listened and realized that Pit Bull possibly gave him enough evidence to identify the murderer who managed to slide under the radar for a long time.

It was getting late, so Draven decided to head home. Little Jimmi was probably worried about him, and Draven did not want to make his dog anxious regarding his whereabouts. Draven thanked Pit Bull for his hospitality and assistance with the case and proceeded to drive himself home. Draven made it home in twenty minutes due to traffic being light and immediately picked up his dog from his neighbor's apartment where he was being dogsat. He took Little Jimmi home and fed him. After that, Little Jimmi and Draven passed out together in the bed from exhaustion.

CHAPTER 73

Detective Overstreet awoke the following day to Little Jimmi's barking. He went to the refrigerator and pulled out the homemade rice-and- carrot dinner that Draven had made for Little Jimmi earlier in the week. Little Jimmi devoured it in seconds, Draven wondered if he inhaled his food. Little Jimmi was a fast eater, and Draven could not understand the rationale behind this behavior. He was fed, at least, three times a day yet seemed like he was constantly hungry and always starving. Little Jimmi seemed to have an obsession with food and eating and went crazy when it was around.

Draven turned on the television set and proceeded to watch a special report on Frontline News stating that the twentieth anniversary of the Great Bayview explosion and fire that took place in San Franciso was almost here. Draven listened as the reporter described the circumstances that led to the explosion and fire and outlined the steps that were taken to rebuild the neighborhood after that. He listened as the reporter described the people who were killed in the fire as well as the damage done in the outlying area complete with pictures in graphic detail. Detective Overstreet watched the entire special and, after it was done, proceeded to get ready for work.

CHAPTER 74

The killer looked around at the frantic activity that was occurring in the office today. People were running around, and they seemed to be in a hurry. They appeared stressed out and impatient with one another. The killer saw his supervisor screaming at the other two workers near his cubicle. He watched as they sprang to their feet and rushed over to see what the boss wanted. The killer saw the two workers run to take care of whatever mundane, pointless task the supervisor was demanding them to complete as if it was the end of the world.

The killer thought to himself, *These other workers are like castrated ponies, and they always rush to the boss like scared, neutered dogs whenever she calls. She seems to have the power of life and death over them.* He again mused to himself, *I wonder how it is to be a lapdog and know that your balls are in your supervisor's purse?* He laughed silently to himself as he thought of everyone cowering before the authority of the so-called boss.

The killer then went back to work and thought to himself, *It is almost time for another victim, and who is this unlucky person?* He continued looking at the screen and focused on his work so he did not have to interact with his supervisor. He thought she was an idiot and a pain in the ass. The killer had nothing but contempt for her and thought she was a prime example of a useless human being. He wondered if she knew how much he hated her and thought, *Probably not. She seemed oblivious to everyone and everything around her and caught up in the next mundane, useless task that needed to be completed in this embarrassment of a job.*

He continued looking at the computer screen and searching for his latest victim. He finally settled on one and mused to himself, *She is local.* After that, he went to YouTube and selected "Nessun

Dorma" by Luciano Pavarotti and became lost in the music. The orchestra was beautiful and singing spectacular. He could hear the music and singer's voice meld together until it led to an epic crescendo. *A pure piece of music,* the killer thought to himself. The killer again mused to himself, *They do not make music like this anymore, and most are overproduced crap today where the person cannot sing.* He looked on the screen and saw the victim's picture once more before turning it off. A smile flashed on his face, and he said, "Soon, very soon, we shall meet."

CHAPTER 75

Detective Overstreet decided that he needed to talk to the supervisor at the Social Security Administration on Kearney Street about other individuals who had access to both applicants' personal records. He knew that the killer had access to this information and needed to know what linked the victims together. Based on what Pit Bull told Draven earlier, it had to do with the blood type of each victim. Draven gathered that each victim had the same blood type, and he wanted to verify this for himself. The only way that Draven could do this was to see it for himself via the victims' personal records at the Social Security Administration.

Draven showered, dressed, and went to the Social Security Administration Building on Kearney Street. Upon entering, he was greeted by a security guard. He flashed his badge at the security guard and introduced himself. Draven requested to speak to the supervisor and said it was official police business. The security guard proceeded to escort Draven to the supervisor's office, but Draven thanked the guard for his assistance and said that he could find it himself.

Detective Overstreet proceeded to walk to the supervisor's office. He seemed to walk for an eternity and wondered if the supervisor had moved his office. He muttered to himself, "It seems like a maze that never ends. I do not remember it being this long."

Draven finally arrived at the supervisor's office, and he saw that this individual was talking to another person on the phone. He sat on the bench outside the supervisor's office and waited for him to finish his call. The wait seemed to be forever, but he killed the time by reviewing the questions that he wanted to ask the supervisor pertaining to the unsolved murders.

The supervisor finally finished his call and saw that Detective Overstreet was outside his office. He wondered what Detective Overstreet wanted and opened the door to let him in. Draven thanked the supervisor for seeing him on short notice and proceeded to inform the supervisor that he needed access again to the archived records in the main computer located in the basement. Draven went on to inform the supervisor that the killer was accessing the same information and possibly selecting his victims based on their blood types. He also informed the supervisor that he had reason to believe that the killer was another employee at the Social Security Administration.

The supervisor was floored, and he decided to cooperate with the investigation. He wanted the publicity about the killer possibly being an employee of this administration to go away and was worried that he could really be currently working at this branch.

The supervisor had hired most of the employees who worked at this branch and took pride in being able to screen out people who did not fit the mold that he was trying to establish at this facility. The supervisor wanted hardworking and ethical workers. He did not want employees who abused their right to access personal information of applicants and use it for nefarious purposes. He knew that a scandal of that magnitude could destroy his reputation and ensure that he never worked in this town again.

CHAPTER 76

Detective Overstreet listened as Mr. Sampson called his assistant into the office and informed her that he was granting him access to the archived records. He noticed the same Leslie James, who assisted him before, came into the office. He could sense that she was staring at him and undressing him with her eyes. Draven was flattered but would never cheat on Asia, as he loved her deeply. Asia was the woman he had waited years for, and he would never throw her love away.

Draven watched as Leslie James escorted him to the basement. He watched as she performed the same protocol to enter the room that housed the main computer with the database that contained the archived records. Draven looked on as Leslie James set up the screen so he could search for the requested information. When this was done, Draven thanked her for her assistance, and she left the room.

Draven began his online search. He pulled out his notepad that had the names of all the victims and started with Trish Armstrong. He typed her name into the computer and pulled up the information pertaining to her demographics.

The information came up, and he went to the section called Blood Type. He noticed it said AB-. Draven did the same for Lisa Miranda and noticed that she also had AB- as her blood type. He did the same for the other victims and achieved the same results. Draven then said to himself, "That is the key. They all have AB- as their blood type. That is the connection."

Draven went to the section marked Sorting and put in the information so the computer could highlight all applications that had Blood Type AB-. He watched as the microprocessors began to process this request. Immediately, the computer sent out five more names, and he jotted them down in his notebook, along with their home addresses and telephone numbers.

Before logging off, he looked up the names of the individuals who processed these applications and noticed there were three different names. Draven thought to himself, *One of these individuals has to be the killer, and I just need to find their blood type*. Draven then proceeded to log off the computer and went to see Mr. Sampson so he could explain this situation to him.

CHAPTER 77

Detective Overstreet went to speak with Walter Sampson about the case. He, once again, entered the labyrinthian maze of the hallway that led to Mr. Sampson's office but this time did not get lost. It was close though, but he was able to remember the path that led to it. Draven was relieved about that because he was eager to talk to Mr. Sampson pertaining to the employee who had access to the archived files in the computer database.

Draven arrived at the office of Mr. Walter Sampson. Detective Overstreet began to explain his findings in the case and emphasized the fact that the killer was choosing his victims based on their blood type and targeted those who were AB-. He then requested information as to the identity of the individuals who had access to that and listened as Mr. Sampson relayed the information to Draven.

"All the employees have access to this information because they perform various functions at one time or another," Mr. Sampson said. "At more than one time or another, each employee has had to upload files into the main database in the basement of this building or audit them."

Draven listened intently but became flustered inside and thought to himself, *That is a huge pool of people that we need to investigate and screen.* Draven then responded by saying, "Can we also check the files of the employees as to see who has a blood type of AB-?

Mr. Sampson said, "I would need a court order before that request could be granted due to the delicate nature of it."

Draven responded by saying, "I will get this order, believe me, so this process could begin as soon as possible. We have a madman on the loose, and we need to apprehend him immediately before he hurts another person or ruins another family."

After Detective Overstreet left, Mr. Sampson thought, *Here we go again. The police department is targeting my employees, and they are going to be the ruin of me.* He could not believe that this was happening but felt he better not interfere with an ongoing police investigation because that could make matters worse. He thought it best to cooperate and not rock the boat.

CHAPTER 78

The killer saw Detective Overstreet enter the Social Security Administration Building on Kearney Street and go directly to speak to Mr. Walter Sampson, lead supervisor for this branch. He knew that it was important because heads of various departments were in the room while Draven was speaking and the door was closed. The killer saw Detective Overstreet walk into the supervisor's office as if a huge break had occurred in the case and he needed to share it with other people immediately. He watched as Draven did all the talking and everyone else listened and nodded in agreement.

The killer watched as Draven exited the building in a huge hurry as if to take care of an important matter. He thought, *I love to see self- important people move in a hurry to take care of an urgent matter as if nothing else matters.* He then saw as the section chief started, once again, yelling at two employees who worked in the cubicles next to him. He could see that his section chief was extremely frustrated with these two employees and looked visibly red with anger. She looked like she was going to have a heart attack because a profuse amount of sweat was pouring down her face and her face became redder the more frustrated she became with these two employees. Her voice was loud, and it seemed the section chief was beginning to feel as if the anger was taking control of her body.

The killer thought that she was going to have a coronary heart attack in the office any moment. He watched as the lead supervisor, Walter Sampson, talked to the section chief, and with some effort, she was able to calm down and go back to work. The killer marveled at the demeanor of Mr. Walter Sampson because he was able to calm her down, regardless of the presenting problem or her temperament. That was Mr. Sampson's gift, and he admired it.

CHAPTER 79

Detective Overstreet went to the office of the Honorable Oliver Wendell Whitehurst to obtain a search warrant. He was able to reach the judge's office in a short amount of time. He noticed that the judge's office was at 400 McAllister Street in the Federal building, and parking proved to be a nightmare. They did not have a parking lot near the building, so he was forced to park on the street. He thought that this would be a challenge because the streets were narrow and it was going to be a tight squeeze.

Draven was able to park his car and proceeded to the federal building, which he noticed was a gray, sterile structure, devoid of any plants and elaborate decorations. It was made of solid steel and had huge iron doors, which were a challenge to open. They led into a huge hall with security guards who instructed Draven to place all metal objects into a tray before walking into a scanner. Draven listened as the security guards informed him that this was a safety precaution. Detective Overstreet watched as they told him to pick up his personal items on the other side once they had been scanned and screened for possible weapons. Draven informed them that the purpose of his visit was to speak to the Honorable Oliver Wendell Whitehurst about securing a search warrant. While doing this, Draven flashed his badge to the security guards and identified himself as Detective Overstreet from the San Francisco Police Department.

Detective Overstreet observed the behavior of the security guards as they went through the process to screen his personal items for possible weapons before taking the elevator to the judge's office. He saw that they were professional, stern, and direct when communicating various parts of protocol pertaining to screening personal property while individuals entered the Federal building. He noticed that the security guards wore a uniform and carried guns and that despite their rough exterior and demeanor, they were easy to speak to and generally passionate about their job, keeping everyone at the Federal building safe. Draven also reminded himself that there were judges working in that building and the security guards were responsible for their safety as well.

After completing the safety protocol, he requested the office number for the Honorable Oliver Wendell Whitehurst and listened as one of the security guards relayed this information to him. Draven thanked the guard for his assistance and approached the elevator so he could take it to the fourth floor.

Detective Overstreet waited for an eternity for the elevator to open up after selecting the appropriate button. He thought, *Why do elevators in federal buildings and hospitals take a long time to open up?* It seemed like this always happens, and it baffled Draven. Other people were waiting next to Draven for the elevator, and he could tell that they were having the same responses. He could feel some people breathing faster and mumbling to themselves the longer the elevator took to open. Draven saw one individual becoming redder as his anger intensified and thought that this person was going to have a heart attack. This person started doing breathing exercises to calm down, and his face began turning back to its normal color. Draven was relieved because he did not want anyone to experience cardiac arrest in the hallway. Waiting for the elevator was an annoyance, and Draven thought it was not worth losing a life over.

CHAPTER 80

The elevator finally opened up, and the crowd was relieved. People piled in and proceeded to press the buttons of the floors they wanted to go to. Draven selected the button indicating the fourth floor and watched as the elevator shot up like a bullet. He could feel the fast and jerky motion playing havoc with his stomach. He thought again to himself, *How can some elevators go up and down really fast while others do not?* This was a question Draven had, and he never seemed to get a definite answer. There were many theories but no definite answer to this question.

Detective Overstreet stood at the back of the elevator and waited for it to reach the fourth floor. He was eager to reach the fourth floor because the music in the background was irritating him. It was soft rock, but Draven could not ascertain the name of the song and artist who sang it and only knew that he did not care for the song. The elevator was cramped full of people, and movement was next to impossible. He counted the seconds that it took the elevator to reach the fourth floor because the heater was on full blast, which made it difficult, if not impossible, to breath. It finally arrived at the fourth floor, and Draven practically ran out of the elevator. He almost kissed the ground but thought, *I have business to attend to and need to get a hold of myself.*

CHAPTER 81

Detective Overstreet made it to the office of the Honorable Oliver Wendell Whitehurst. Before going in, he reviewed his notebook that had salient points about the case that he wanted to relay to the judge pertaining to the request for a search warrant. When done, he took a deep breath and made an inspection of the clothes that he was wearing. Draven wanted to make sure that he was neatly dressed and well-groomed before speaking to the judge. He did his research on the judge and knew that this individual was a stickler for proper attire at the workplace. Draven knew that meant a suit and tie, which he wore today.

Draven walked in and noticed that the reception area was immense. On the right side of the room, a desk stood, and behind it was an administrative assistant whose job was to buzz people in to see the judge. The judge was in the next room. Nearby were seats that people could sit on while waiting. The walls of the reception area were painted beige, and they had pictures of national landmarks in San Francisco on them, which included the Golden Gate Bridge and Koit Tower. The floor had beige carpeting, and the reception area was pretty calm and relaxed for a waiting room. Someone could almost fall asleep in it.

Detective Overstreet approached the desk of the administrative assistant and flashed his badge. He introduced himself as Det. Draven Overstreet from the San Francisco Police Department and said that he was there to see the judge about the granting of a search warrant. The administrative assistant introduced herself as Alexis Page, and she requested that Draven have a seat. Then she contacted the Honorable Oliver Wendell Whitehurst via telephone and said, "Sir, Det. Draven Overstreet is here to see you about the granting of a search warrant."

Draven heard the judge mutter a response on the phone, but

he could not understand it. The phone call ended, and Alexis informed Draven that the judge would see him today as soon as possible. Alexia then asked Draven if he wanted something to drink, and Draven responded by saying, "Herbal tea please." She came back with herbal tea, and Draven thanked Alexis for her assistance. He then proceeded to wait to speak to the judge.

CHAPTER 82

Draven thought that the judge would never come. He waited for what seemed like an eternity. Draven poured over the magazines in the reception area hoping that the time waiting to see the judge would go faster. He looked over the notes in his notebook, one last time, to make sure that he remembered what to say when speaking to the judge. Draven knew that sometimes his anxiety heightens when speaking to an authority figure and he could have difficulties remembering everything that he wanted to say to that individual. Draven was about to give up hope pertaining to speaking to the judge and go home when suddenly Alexis Page said, "The judge will see you now."

Draven took a deep breath and walked into the judge's office. He noticed that the heater was on, and walls were covered with photos of the judge with various celebrities, which included former president Barack Obama along with Stephen Curry. There were bookshelves covered with law books and back issues of the *Judicial Review* periodical. Next to one of the bookshelves was a table that had the judge's law degree from Georgetown University, along with an incense burner on it. Draven could smell the fragrance of incense ingulfing the room. He recognized it as Healing and said that it was one of his favorite fragrances. In front of Draven was a desk where a Caucasian male in his fifties was sitting. He recognized this person as the Honorable Oliver Wendell Whitehurst.

The Honorable Oliver Wendell Whitehurst approached Draven and introduced himself to him. Draven shook the judge's hand and introduced himself. The judge then asked Draven to have a seat and proceeded to burn incense. Judge Whitehurst said, "The incense helps relieve stress, and as you know, fighting crime in its many fronts could be fulfilling yet challenging. We need to take necessary precautions to stay in the fight." Draven nodded in agreement and mentioned that he burned incense in his office and residence for the same reason.

After exchanging pleasantries, Draven talked about the judge needing to grant him a search warrant pertaining to employee files at the Social Security Administration office on Kearny Street. He spoke about the killer selecting victims based on the rare blood type AB- and said that the Social Security Administration was one agency where any staff could have access to this information. Draven talked about needing to catch the serial killer and said this could be the big break they needed.

He made a great argument for the search warrant, and in the end, the judge granted it. Detective Overstreet waited while the judge completed the paperwork. This process took an hour, and when it was done, Detective Overstreet thanked the judge for his assistance. Draven then drove to Captain Hammer's office to relay the good news that a search warrant had been granted.

CHAPTER 83

Asia Francisco was excited and could hardly contain herself. She was finally going to take that much needed and deserved vacation to Hawaii. Asia had been to Hawaii before, and she loved everything about it. Asia loved the long walks on the beaches, nightly luaus, hula dancing, and seeing the sun go down without a care in the world. She enjoyed the snorkeling and undersea exploration of the coral reefs. She has seen them before, and they were majestic and captivating. The corals were beautiful and created a harmonious blend, which silhouetted throughout the ocean.

Asia was jumping up and down inside and was eager to start her vacation. She could practically smell and taste everything that was Hawaii, which included two weeks of heavenly, carefree bliss. She knew that when she became excited about anything, it was difficult for her to maintain focus and concentration on the tasks at hand. In this case, these tasks included packing clothing, obtaining all documents needed for travel, and informing staff that she would be gone for two weeks. Asia had already secured an airline ticket for next Thursday and her vacation to Hawaii was finally becoming a reality. She also needed to give the Police Department in San Francisco an advanced notice so they could secure a replacement worker for two weeks while she was on vacation because Asia knew that crime slept for no one.

CHAPTER 84

Draven flew out of the judge's office and headed to Captain Hammer's office. He was excited about finally securing the search warrant. Draven felt relieved that he possessed the one document which could, more than likely, break the case wide open, and he was eager to tell the chief about it. He desperately wanted to close this case and identify and arrest the serial killer before more harm was done to the public.

Draven was on the open road and eager to talk to the chief about the procurement of the search warrant. It was a dark, gray, foggy morning, and traffic was at a standstill. He was stuck in gridlock, and it was moving at a snail's pace. He could feel the frustration welling up inside him and thought that he would explode. Draven decided to put on the radio, and "Gimmie Shelter" by The Rolling Stones was playing. He sang with the radio and watched as the stress seemed to drift away. Congestion loosened, and pretty soon, Draven was streaming through traffic and headed for his destination.

Draven finally reached the police station. He thought that he would never reach his destination because of the heavy traffic. It had been busier than usual, and Draven could not figure out why. There was no sign of an accident, and he figured that there were just to many cars on the road. Anyways, Detective Overstreet decided that he had bigger fish to fry and needed to focus his attention on capturing and apprehending a serial killer on the loose in his city.

He went into the police station, and word about securing the search warrant had proceeded him. The other detectives congratulated Draven, and Captain Hammer had a big smile on his face a mile wide. Captain Hammer was extremely proud of Draven for securing the search warrant and was eager to see him serve it to Walter Sampson at the Social Security Administration building on Kearney Street. Before that could happen, Captain Hammer knew that Draven needed to coordinate with the other detectives to make sure that it was served correctly. The captain knew that this was an important aspect of police work and mistakes during this process had led to crucial evidence being inadmissible during a court proceeding in the past. The captain did not want to see that happen. Many police hours had been spent on this case, and failure was not an option.

Draven called a meeting with the other detectives in one of the conference rooms of the police station. Captain Hammer was present at the meeting and decided that Draven would lead the task force designed and assembled to handle the case. Draven had been handling the case since the beginning and had all the information about it. He also was the detective who had secured the search warrant from the judge and had already built rapport with Walter Sampson.

They were in the conference room for an hour. In the room, they mapped out a strategy for how the search warrant would be served and executed. They decided that another detective would serve the search warrant. Then Draven would begin searching and analyzing the employee files in the database to see who had blood type AB-. Draven also decided that police officers needed to be present throughout this process to keep onlookers and reporters away from him while he analyzed employee files. It was a delicate process, and distractions could not be tolerated. Everyone agreed to this plan, and the meeting was concluded so steps could be taken to put this plan into action.

CHAPTER 85

Detective Overstreet and the rest of the task force headed for the Social Security Administration building located on Kearney Street. When they arrived, they were greeted by a security guard. Draven noticed that a different guard was on duty today, and he did not recognize him. Detective Overstreet flashed the guard his badge and introduced himself. "I am Det. Draven Overstreet from the San Francisco Police Department. The other individuals present are part of a task force organized by the San Francisco Police Department, and they are here to assist me with executing the search warrant."

The guard said, "I need to speak to Mr. Sampson about this."

Detective Overstreet asked, "Is Mr. Sampson in today?"

And the guard responded, "Yes." Draven and the rest of the task force watched as the guard said, "Please follow me to Mr. Sampson's office."

Detective Overstreet declined and said, "I know where it is." They watched as the guard left. Draven and the rest of the task force proceeded to walk in the long, dark hallway toward Mr. Walter Sampson's office.

They reached his office and knocked on the door. He answered and was greeted by Draven and the rest of the task force. He presented Mr. Sampson with the search warrant and watched as he signed the document after reading it. He then watched as Mr. Sampson contacted his administrative assistant, via telephone, and asked that Draven, along with the rest of the task force, be escorted to the room in the basement to view the database that housed the archived records. The administrative assistant proceeded to do this, and Draven noticed that a different person was escorting them to their destination. Draven asked about the whereabouts of the previous administrative assistant, Ms. James.

He was informed that she no longer worked for this agency and moved back to New York. Draven was surprised but gathered that this position at the SSA had a high turnover rate.

Detective Overstreet watched as Ms. Helen Garcia scanned her card to allow him and the rest of task force access to the room. Draven watched as Ms. Garcia completed the protocols required for him to view the requested information on the computer. When done, Ms. Garcia informed Det. Overstreet that the system was ready for usage. He thanked her for her assistance and watched as she proceeded to exit the room. He was thankful that Ms. Garcia was not going to stay in the room and watch as he viewed the database. That would make the situation extremely awkward and uncomfortable.

CHAPTER 86

Draven poured over the records in the database. He searched each employment record on the database in a meticulous fashion. Draven made a careful note of each employee with the AB- blood type and placed the information in his notebook, along with other employee- related information, which included their home address, contact numbers, and position held in the company. He planned to interview these people at a later date after he had viewed all information in the database.

Detective Overstreet had to take various breaks throughout the process. The room was cramped, and the constant sitting was starting to make his back lock up. Draven was in constant lower-back pain due to marches he attended in the past for various causes, which included LGBT and Women's Rights, as well as the ending of the war in Iraq. At these marches, he had been physically attacked by the police, and his body had never fully healed. To this day, he was in constant pain and used gummies and physical therapy to relieve it.

Detective Overstreet went outside to take a break. The room was hot due to the computer being on and working at a frantic pitch. He spoke to the officers who were preventing reporters and other people from entering this room, "How are you holding up?"

One of the officers said, "People have been following our commands to not attempt to enter this room, but most of us are getting tired."

Draven could tell that they were getting exhausted, so he walked next door to Starbucks to purchase coffee for them as token of gratitude. He brought several mochas and two lattes and took them back to the police officers. He presented the coffee to the officers, and they thanked him. They were extremely grateful because someone took the time and acknowledged the work that was being done. It was a hard and, sometimes, thankless job, but someone needed to keep the streets and the public safe from the local vermin.

CHAPTER 87

Detective Overstreet finally completed analyzing all the records in the database. It was quite an ordeal, and Draven was exhausted. His body ached from the constant sitting, and he was in desperate need of a gummy and deep tissue massage. He could feel the nerves in his lower back acting up and pain receptors firing at a fever pitch. The pain was worse than usual, but Draven could psychologically block it out and focus on the task at hand. In this case, the task at hand was capturing a serial killer who was elusive and proved to be one step ahead of the police at all times.

Detective Overstreet went into one of the conference rooms at the Social Security Administration building, and he reviewed the list of suspects that he gathered from examining the database. The first suspect was Jeremiah Parker. He was an African American male and in his twenties. He worked as a data analyst for the Social Security Administration and had been doing this for ten years. The second suspect was Eileen Comstock. She was a Caucasian female in her thirties and section chief for the auditing division at the SSA for ten years. The last suspect was Joe Johnstone, also a data analyst. He was a Caucasian male and had been working in this agency for five years.

Draven looked over this list and thought to himself, *One of these individuals is the killer, yet that doesn't seem right.* Draven had been doing police work for several years and had a sixth sense for the outcome of an investigation. Even before speaking to these people, he felt that they did not fit the mold of someone who could perpetrate these killings. The killer had an aura about him, and none of these people appeared to have that. He decided that he needed to do all the follow-up work before fully giving into this hunch.

CHAPTER 88

The killer was watching all the activity at the Social Security Administration office. He watched as Det. Overstreet and the other officers spoke to Mr. Walter Sampson in his office. He noticed that Draven, once again, did all the talking and Mr. Sampson just listened. He noticed that they were in his office for a long time and observed that Draven spoke in a calm but professional manner. He never seemed out of control and always appeared to have command of the situation.

The killer watched how Mr. Sampson seemed calm and relaxed throughout his interactions with the police. He did not raise his voice or become angry. Mr. Sampson did not appear to become sweaty when talking to the police or fidget with his hands. He spoke in an assertive but professional manner when interacting with the police and never garbled his words. He seemed in command at all times, and the killer started to wonder, *Has Mr. Sampson had a run-in with the police before? Most people are nervous when they deal with the police, but not Mr. Sampson. He has a calm and controlled demeanor about himself.*

The killer always respected Mr. Sampson. Mr. Sampson had arranged for the killer to work for this agency and treated him like a son. He looked out for the killer and tried to keep him away from the section chief. The section chief could be a real micromanager, and in the past, this caused people to quit. Mr. Sampson did not want to see that happen. The killer was a great worker, kept to himself, and did not create problems at work, which Mr. Sampson appreciated.

CHAPTER 89

Detective Overstreet went to see the three suspects who work at the SSI office on Kearney Street. He spoke to all three individuals concerning their whereabouts on the nights of the murders. Draven listened as they presented this information to him and placed it in his notebook for further review at a later date. They watched as he gathered information pertaining to witnesses who could verify the location of the suspects on the night of the murders and looked on as this was placed into his notebook as well. Draven hoped that one of these suspects was the killer. He wanted the case solved and the killer finally brought to justice. He did not like the fact that someone was targeting women in his hometown and felt helpless about being unable to stop it. Draven took that extremely personal and, more than ever, wanted to apprehend and nail the killer.

The case was having a profound effect on Draven, and this was starting to bother him. Draven was having problems sleeping and experienced the same reoccurring nightmare. The dream started out the same way every night. Draven was in a long, dark, gray, tunnel and could hear a woman screaming in the background. Draven could never ascertain the identity of this individual. He would start walking, and suddenly, the lights would come on, which illuminated the tunnel. The tunnel was dirty, and at the far end, he would see a figure enter an open door. The figure was unrecognizable, and then Draven would run toward this individual. But before that happened, Draven would notice the files of the victims on the floor covered in blood. When touching the files, he would get blood all over his hands, and it would not come off, despite his efforts to do so.

When going into the open door, Draven would enter a room. In the room, Asia's dead body would be wrapped in plastic and drained of all her blood. A note would be on the plastic covering, saying, "You will never catch me." At this time, Draven would start screaming, and it would awaken him from a sound sleep. Sweat would be pouring down his face and his heart beating rapidly. Draven would be completely disoriented, and Little Jimmi usually came to comfort and calm Draven down. This whole process would take several hours, but Draven would eventually go back to sleep.

CHAPTER 90

Asia came to visit Draven at work. She was excited and could hardly contain herself. Asia spoke really fast and was a fireball of energy that had no bounds. She started talking about her upcoming yearly trip to Hawaii. Asia began describing the activities that she would participate in while on her trip. This included swimming, walking on the beaches, undersea corral exploration, luaus, and deep-tissue, morning massages. It sounded like tropical paradise and full experience of relaxation.

Detective Overstreet knew that Asia needed this vacation and a break from the daily grind of work. She worked over forty hours a week and frequently worked several days in a row with little-to-no sleep. Asia had to process numerous amounts of evidence that never seemed to end. This included mountains of paperwork and numerous agents she needed to consult with and relay her findings to. It was a time-consuming, cumbersome, and exhausting job that Asia loved but needed a respite from at times.

Detective Overstreet listened as Asia talked about all the tasks she needed to complete before her vacation started. This included packing clothing, obtaining official identification, making hotel reservations, and informing her supervisor in the forensics department that she would be gone from work for two weeks. Draven listened further as Asia talked about completing some of these tasks already and hoping to finish the remainder of them by the end of the week.

Asia could see that the police station was becoming increasingly busy and frantic, so she decided it was better they talk later in the day. She knew that the case pertaining to the serial killer had everyone working overtime and following up on numerous leads. She knew that Draven had other cases to handle besides the unsolved serial killings and he needed to focus all his efforts on them. With that, she decided to let Draven get back to work and made plans to see him later that day for dinner.

When leaving the police station, Asia thought about the conversation that they had about work. During the conversation, Asia noticed that Draven looked exhausted and was in dire need of relaxation. His face was sunk, and he was ready to fall asleep at his desk. He could barely keep his eyes open, and he was wearing the same clothes that he had on yesterday. Asia thought, *Draven is sleeping at the office and working on the case nonstop. I bet that he has not had a homecooked meal in ages and lives of food from vending machines at the police station.* Asia then decided that she would make Draven his favorite homecooked meal: spaghetti and meatballs with a bottle of red wine tonight.

CHAPTER 91

Draven spent the rest of the day following up on various leads provided by the suspects that he spoke to earlier in the conference room. He contacted each of the witnesses that the suspects provided via telephone concerning their whereabouts on the nights of the murders and listened as each alibi checked out. When done, Draven was getting that irritated, frustrated feeling in the pit of his stomach that none of these suspects was the killer. His original hunch had been proven correct, and he did not have a clue as to what the next steps in the investigation were. Draven was truly without any direction pertaining to solving the case, and this frustrated him.

Detective Overstreet proceeded to the conference room where the task force was working diligently around the clock, and he broke the news to them. "All the suspects' alibis had checked out, and because of that, we are back at ground zero." The other detectives were dumbfounded, and their mouths were wide open in disbelief. They were in a state of shock, and a pin drop could be heard in the room.

There was an uncomfortable silence throughout the room, and the captain's facial expression said all that was needed. "The killings will continue, and we do not have a goddamn clue as to how to stop it."

Draven exited the conference room and proceeded to his desk. He looked at the case files, and he was speechless. He could not believe that none of these suspects panned out as being the killer. Draven was so sure that the killer worked at the Social Security Administration on Kearney Street and thought, *What was I missing? I followed all the clues and evidence, and it led me to this location.* Draven continued staring at the case files as if they would subconsciously relay the next course of action pertaining to solving the case and apprehending the killer to him. This continued, for at least, thirty minutes, until Draven decided that this was ludicrous and not helping to resolve the situation. "I am going to eventually catch the killer, and I just need to keep working on the case," Draven said to himself. In the meantime, he was going to enjoy a great dinner and date at Asia's house. He worked hard and deserved it.

CHAPTER 92

Before proceeding to Asia's house, Draven decided to go home and take a warm shower. He had been working nonstop on the case for the past forty-eight hours, and he reeked and his muscles ached from all the tension he housed in his body. While showering, he could feel his muscles unclench and the rest of his body relax. The nice, warm water worked its magic and caused all the stress engulfing his body to evaporate like water on a sweltering, muggy day. This was exactly what he needed before spending a magical night with the love of his life, Asia Francisco.

When done with his shower, Draven dried off and went to select his wardrobe for the evening. He wanted to wear something special for Asia, considering it was their first official date and night together as a couple. He selected an all-black suit with a bloody-red tie. Draven thought the suit was perfect for the evening, and it blended the best of both worlds, a nice suit with Gothic overtones, which was his style. He selected his shoes and dropped off Little Jimmi with his next-door neighbor for the night. He had a feeling that it would be a late evening.

Draven got in his car and proceeded to head to Asia's house. On the way over, he selected a beautiful bouquet of red roses along with a bottle of Chianti. He thought it only fair to bring a present as a thank you to the woman of his dreams who welcomed him and his heart into her life. He had been waiting years for this person, and she had finally arrived. He also wrote a beautiful sentiment in the card to remind Asia that a gentle but caring heart lay behind that badge.

Draven parked his car and headed to Asia's residence. It was a beautiful black and red–painted house in the Seacliff District of San Francisco. It had a huge lawn filled with a lush garden full of a wide assortment of plants. These plants included roses, tulips, and a whole menagerie of various beautifully manicured flowers. In front of the house, stood a massive white marble statue of an angel, and a welcome sign lay on the porch. A red Mustang with lightning bolts at the ends of the two doors stood parked in the driveway. It looked like a house from a *Better Homes and Gardens* magazine.

CHAPTER 93

Draven approached the door to Asia's residence and rang the doorbell. The doorbell went off, and he could hear a familiar song echoing throughout the house. He immediately recognized it as "Gimmie Shelter" by The Rolling Stones. Draven heard footsteps approach the door, and a familiar voice said, "Who's there?"

Draven replied, "It is me, your knight in shining armor."

The door burst open, and Asia stood before him like a majestic beauty that had no other rival. She wore a long black dress with black fishnet stockings. Asia had several silver rings on her fingers and red highlights in her black hair. Asia's long hair was streaming down her neck as if inviting Draven into her house for acts of erotic seduction, which would take place later that day. Draven was completely enamored by her beauty and felt her love for Asia growing into a mighty majestic crescendo that had no equal.

Asia invited Draven into her house, and he could smell the sweet aroma of sausage with spaghetti sauce engulfing his senses. His mouth was watering at the smells that were enveloping his nose, and hunger began consuming Draven to the point that he would, gladly, eat his own arm if needed, to sustain himself. But Draven knew he had to wait because perfection takes time to achieve. Asia was famous for her homemade spaghetti with meatballs, mushrooms, and sweet Italian sausage. Word traveled around the office about Asia's premier talent for making Italian food that could take someone's breath away and soothe the savage beast of unsatiable hunger.

Asia invited Draven to sit down on the couch and offered him a glass of wine he had brought them for dinner. But before taking a sip of it, he presented the bouquet of red roses he bought earlier to Aisa, and she melted. She loved the roses and immediately placed them in a vase with water. Then they continued talking until the food was ready. Throughout the conversation, Draven kept thinking about Asia's famous spaghetti and could barely contain himself when the food finally came.

Draven was salivating. He could smell the sweet aroma overcoming his senses and preparing him for a cornucopia of erotic food pleasure. He placed the noodles in his mouth and was instantly transported to food heaven and nirvana. The pasta was a perfect match with the sweet Italian sausage, a majestic touch to a magical meal. The sweet sourdough bread rounded out this heavenly experience and placed his tastebuds on overload. Dessert was Tiramisu with whip cream, and Draven could barely move after consuming all this food. He was full, but his stomach was pleased and body at rest.

It was getting late and dark outside. Draven still had a thirty-minute drive back to his apartment, but Asia had other plans. The wine had relaxed Asia, and she was completely turned on sexually, ready for the next adventure with the mighty Draven and his long whip, which he had tucked into his pants all evening. Asia gave Draven the look requesting to have a conversation with the trouser python in his pants. They both went into Asia's room and several hours later, after heart- pounding thrusts and thunderous performances in bed, he emerged from it. Draven smoked a cigarette, while Asia remained knocked out. Several minutes later, Asia awoke and said, "This was an experience that I will never forget, and you truly are a mighty beast in bed." With that, Draven decided to spend the night and the next morning with Asia.

CHAPTER 94

Draven awoke early in the morning and decided to make Asia a homemade breakfast. It was a warm, sunny morning without a cloud in the sky. There was a slight breeze in the air, and it had the look of a beautiful day. The hummingbirds were singing and the sparrows chirping as if telling Asia to wake up so she could take full advantage of this precious gift, a beautiful day outdoors.

Draven headed to the kitchen and began to prepare breakfast. He had been a short-order cook in college and was a master of making a quick but tasty meal without messing the kitchen up. He began making eggs and cooking bacon and hash browns. He knew that the trick to cooking bacon and hash browns entailed making sure that they both turned out crispy while remembering to add ketchup to the hash browns. That gave it some added zest. When they were all done, he made freshly squeezed orange juice and left a note on Asia's pillow telling her to meet him outside on the porch.

Asia came down the stairs and went onto the porch. She sat at the table and marveled at the feast that lay before her. It looked tasty, and she could hardly wait to dive in. She tried the bacon and eggs first. Her tastebuds were immediately overwhelmed with a tapestry of flavor that tasted majestic. The hash browns with ketchup completed this menagerie of opulence, and she washed it down with a cool glass of homemade orange juice.

Asia looked at all the flowers at the garden overlooking the patio while she felt the sun illuminating it. She could hear the hummingbirds singing and the sparrows chirping as they greeted the couple this morning. Asia could see the raccoons and squirrels playing in the garden. She realized that there was not a single cloud in the sky and a gentle breeze was blowing in the background. It had the making of a beautiful day, and Draven wanted to take full advantage of it.

CHAPTER 95

After eating breakfast, Draven decided to watch the morning news on Channel 2. It had been years since he watched the morning news. Draven usually woke up early in the morning and got ready for work, which started at eight. He barely had time for breakfast and usually ended up buying a donut and coffee at the local bakery located a block away from the police station. This had been Draven's routine for the last twenty years, and it was nice to take a break from it. Draven felt that it was getting old and tiresome.

The big story in the morning news was the upcoming twenty-year- old anniversary of the Great Bayview explosion along with subsequent fire. Draven was a teenager when it happened but remembered the impact that it had on him personally. One of his close childhood friends was killed in the explosion that started the fire. Listening to the special news report caused memories of his loss to come back but he decided to watch it. He thought it would help him make peace with his loss and allow him to continue the mourning process.

Draven listened as the newscaster relayed the story about the Great Bayview explosion along with subsequent fire to the captive audience watching on television. He started by talking about the shootout in the meth lab at the Bayview/Hunter's Point District in San Francisco that caused an explosion and led to a massive fire engulfing the entire area in a blaze of destruction. Draven watched as the newscaster showed pictures of people killed in the explosion and subsequent fire and documented efforts that were undertaken to rebuild the area from the carnage. He watched as a panoramic view was shown to document the damage done by this disaster and the cleanup that resulted in the newly constructed Bayview/Hunter's Point District.

CHAPTER 96

The killer sat at his desk, and a huge smile flashed across his face. He watched as the police bungled through another investigation and laughed inside quietly to himself. He wondered how most of them drew a paycheck and thought about how he was able to outwit and outthink them at each turn. It was like watching a master chess player face amateurs who were clueless about how their pieces worked on a chessboard. He continued to remain a step ahead of them, and they failed to see that the killer was right under their noses. He said internally to himself, *I am here, and I dare you to catch me.*

The killer continued to enjoy the cat-and-mouse game that he was playing with the police department. *I have them tripping over themselves and bungling through the case in a haphazard way. They have the evidence in front of them and cannot connect the dots to apprehend me. I have proven myself better than Dahmer, Ramirez, Bundy, and Gacy because they all got caught in the end. I won't, and that kills the police inside. I will never see the halls of justice no matter how hard they try.*

The killer decided to get back to work and focus on his job. He did not want to be seen or noticed by the police who were busy following up on leads at the Social Security Administration on Kearney Street. That would bring attention and put the spotlight on him. He wanted to be a chameleon and blend into the crowd while silently laughing to himself about the disaster of an investigation that was unfolding around him.

CHAPTER 97

Draven decided to spend his Saturday with Asia and Little Jimmi. He would take them on a picnic at the park. Before doing that, he decided to go to Lunardi's Market to buy hamburger meat and potato salad for the outdoor barbecue that he was going to have at Golden Gate Park later that day. He selected other items and placed them in his shopping cart. Draven paid for these items, and Asia assisted him with loading them into his car. Draven headed to his neighbor's apartment to get Little Jimmi.

He knocked on the door and could hear Little Jimmi barking loudly as if begging to be released from his current enclosure. The neighbor opened the door, and Little Jimmi burst out ingulfing Draven in a blitzkrieg of love via massive licking. Asia was with Draven, so when Little Jimmi was done licking Draven, he ran toward Asia, requesting a warm embrace. She put Little Jimmi in her arms, thanked the neighbor for watching him, and went to enjoy their magical day at the park together.

They arrived at Golden Gate Park, and it was a gorgeous, majestic day. The sun was shining, and the smell of freshly cut grass echoed throughout the park. The hummingbirds were singing, and the raccoons and squirrels were playing carefree on the grass. The fish were in the pond with all their menagerie of colors, and a slight breeze enveloped the air. Today was a gift, and Draven was going to spend it with his two best friends in the world: the woman of his dreams and his most loyal companion who would never leave him no matter what. He thought this truly was heaven.

Draven ramped up the barbecue pit and started preparing the brickettes. While this was going on, he pulled out his portable CD player and put on "The Last Beat of My Heart" by Siouxsie and the Banshees. He asked Asia to dance with him, and he was in heaven for those five minutes. The only thing that mattered was their love for each other, and they felt that it could see them through any challenge that life presented. This song meant a lot to them, and after that, it became their song forever.

Draven got completely wrapped up in the moment, He almost forgot about the food. The flames were getting high in the barbecue pit, and he thought that it was time to put the hamburgers on. He did that and let them cook for five minutes on one side. Draven turned them over and did the same. He repeated this pattern until they were done and ready for consumption.

The food was done, and everyone was starving. Draven served the hamburgers and prepared the potato salad. Little Jimmi had his own hamburger and was salivating at it. Everyone dug in, and the taste of barbecue overcame their senses. Nobody spoke or made a sound, and everyone enjoyed their meal. It was washed down with an ice- cold glass of Mug root beer, followed by a slice of German chocolate cake. Little Jimmi had vanilla cake because dogs were allergic to chocolate and it proved to be fatal to them.

CHAPTER 98

The mayor decided to pay a visit to the San Francisco Police Department. He wanted to talk to the detectives and the other police personnel who were handling the case. The mayor wanted details pertaining to actions the police were taking to solve the case and apprehend the killer. This was an election year, and the mayor did not want to be remembered as the man who allowed the citizens of San Francisco to be held hostage by a serial killer.

The mayor had just arrived at the police station and was getting ready to meet with Detective Overstreet and the other individuals who were handling the case in one of the conference rooms. Suddenly, Draven, the mayor, and everyone in the conference room heard a thunderous, loud commotion outside. They looked out the window of the conference room they were in and saw a huge crowd assembled in the parking lot of the police station. Reporters from Channel 4 Kron News were present, and so was a protestor with a megaphone and a huge gathering shouting, "We need to hold the mayor accountable, and he and the police have failed us." The crowd started getting bigger and the protestor with the megaphone louder as they approached the police station. Captain Hammer advised everyone to stay in the building for their own safety.

The mayor said, "Here we go again," and agreed that it was wise to follow the captain's orders.

Police officers streamed out and ordered the crowd to disperse. The protestor with the megaphone started chanting, "Hell, no, we won't go," and the crowd followed suit. The police officers issued the same request, and it was followed up with the same response. The mayor wanted to go outside and quell the situation, but Captain Hammer said no. He advised the mayor that the crowd was getting revved up and could get violent.

Draven and the other individuals in the police station heard a loud explosion outside. They looked out the window of the conference room and saw that someone had set fire to the mayor's car. They saw other individuals taking garbage cans and throwing them at the police station, which resulted in the trash littering the streets. Another set of individuals proceeded to begin spray painting all the other cars in the police parking lot with expletives on them.

Just then, the mayor ordered the SWAT team to begin handling the situation via the Antiriot Squad. Draven knew that this meant tear gas, rubber bullets, batons, shields, flashbang grenades, and broken bones. He knew that this had to be done but felt bad because some of the protestors were peaceful and did not deserve the excessive force that they would soon encounter. Having this documented by Channel 4 Kron News would not help the mayor in his reelection bid. He would be labeled by mainstream media as an uncaring monster, and that was a death sentence in politics.

Draven saw all this unfold around him and could not believe the carnage and utter violence that followed. He watched as the riot squad approached the protesters and began swinging the batons toward their heads, which resulted in blood littering the streets. He heard the sounds of flashbang grenades and people screaming as they ran for cover while the police swarmed them. He heard loud sounds of rubber bullets as they nailed human flesh and, more than likely, did untold damage. It was all over in an instant, and the mayor had a smile on his face as if happy that order had been restored.

Draven was disgusted with the carnage that had unfolded around him. He knew that the protesters who attacked the police station and participated in all this damage needed to be punished. That did not bother him. He was deeply concerned about the frustration that boiled over because of the unsolved murders and resulted in this happening. Most of the protesters were everyday people who probably paid taxes and never broke a law before that day. Now they were going to jail, and their lives were probably ruined. Others were probably peaceful protesters and just got caught up in this monstrosity of a demonstration. More than ever, he wanted to catch this serial killer and remove this vermin from the streets. He promised to himself, along with the citizens of San Francisco, that, as of this moment, it would be done, and nothing was going to stop him. This was his city, and he would not let a monster have control over it. He decided that the time for bold action was now.

CHAPTER 99

Asia attempted to contact Draven via telephone, and she was panic- stricken. Asia was watching the events pertaining to the protest and subsequent riot at the police station as they unfolded on television, and she was worried that Draven got caught up in the crossfire. Asia knew that Draven was working today and became more worried when he would not answer his phone. She thought that he probably lay dying in the cold, uncaring streets, bleeding to death, with no one to save him as he drew his last breath. Asia started crying and could not imagine her life without her Draven.

Asia decided to pull herself together. She had Little Jimmi with her and decided that she needed to be strong for him. He could sense that something was wrong, and she did not want to scare him more that he already was. Little Jimmi was moaning and pacing back and forth as if in total panic mode. He was shaking, and when Asia grabbed him, she noticed that his heart was racing and felt like it was beating out of its chest. She petted and kept saying, "Everything will be okay," as Little Jimmi completely melted in her arms.

CHAPTER 100

Asia tried to be strong for Little Jimmi but deep down feared for Draven's life. She played with Little Jimmi and did her best to comfort him. Asia stroked his black, silky fur and talked to Little Jimmi in a way as to ease his pain. She gave him love and other forms of affection. She used Little Jimmi's toys to play with him, and in an indirect manner, this helped calm her own nerves.

Asia thought Draven would never call her. Minutes seemed like hours that passed slowly and without end. Time dragged, and images of Draven's possible death and suffering spread through her mind like wildfire. It was a raging inferno of constant worry in Asia's head pertaining to Draven's safety, and Asia thought that this was hell on earth.

Draven finally called Asia, and Asia's heart sank. She could barely talk and almost started crying as Draven spoke. She heard Draven say, "I am okay and remained in the police station while the situation unfolded outside." She felt relieved to hear Draven's voice and was ready to drive down to the police station to take him home. Draven advised her not to do this because there were a lot of people who needed medical assistance immediately.

They talked for an hour and spoke about the incident that occurred at the police station. Asia listened as Draven talked about being scared that he would never see her or Little Jimmi again. He talked about wanting to grab her and never let go, forever enveloped in her warm embrace. The incident reminded Draven that the most important people in his life were Asia and Little Jimmi. They were his world, and he needed to hold onto them forever and protect them with his life. When they were done talking, Draven said he was coming home. Asia responded by saying, "I would like that," as Little Jimmi started jumping up and down while Draven spoke over the telephone. Little Jimmi loved Draven deeply and wanted Draven there with him as well.

CHAPTER 101

The mayor called a press conference the following day to discuss the situation that occurred yesterday at the police station. He wanted to talk about it along with the steps that were being taken to prevent a similar incident from occurring in the future. All the local stations would be carrying the press conference, plus CNN, MSNBC, and Fox News. Draven, along with the rest of the San Francisco Police Department, were advised to attend the press conference, which would be held outside city hall tomorrow at ten. It was also open to the public.

It was a warm, sunny, beautiful day the following day, and not a cloud was to be seen in the sky. The air was crisp, and the press arrived an hour early to start setting up their equipment. The police had also arrived and began searching for bombs and any other signs of terrorist activity. Staff members assisted with setting up tables and other components vital to the press conference. The police also began scanning credentials of the press to make sure that these individuals were who they claimed to be. Barricades were erected to separate the mayor and his staff from the general public. Nobody wanted a repeat of the events that occurred yesterday with the mayor, and all steps were being taken to prevent this from occurring.

Draven and Asia attended the press conference. They both lived and grew up in San Francisco and wanted information pertaining to the steps that the mayor was taking to prevent future altercations similar to yesterday from occurring. They left Little Jimmi with their neighbor at Draven's apartment because they both thought a similar incident might occur today and did not want Little Jimmi to get caught up in it. They both wanted to keep him safe.

They both arrived at City Hall thirty minutes before the press conference started. They flashed the police officers their credentials but still had to go through all security protocol to enter the enclosure where the mayor would soon speak. They emptied their pockets, and Aisa had her purse searched by the police. When done, they entered the enclosure where the mayor would speak shortly and sat down. Draven made sure Asia was seated first before himself. After all, he was a gentleman and wanted to make sure his girlfriend knew that.

CHAPTER 102

The mayor arrived at the press conference, and his staff began escorting him to the podium so he could address the crowd. The crowd was quiet and watched as the mayor began speaking. He opened his speech by thanking the San Francisco Police Department and other individuals for helping make the event possible. He also thanked the San Francisco Board of Supervisors, former California senator Nancy Pelosi, and other dignitaries attending this event.

The mayor then began talking about the situation that occurred yesterday at the San Francisco Police Station parking lot. He thanked the San Francisco Police Department for their assistance in quelling the situation and keeping individuals safe from bodily harm. Before proceeding any further, he reminded the reporters gathered today that questions would be taken after the press conference.

Then a loud voice pierced the press conference. The protestor with the bullhorn was back, and a crowd stood behind her. She started screaming, "A killer is on the loose in our city, and your solution is to arrest and attack people voicing their disappointment in you. Impeach him now." The police officers swarmed at the lady with the bullhorn and proceeded to arrest her.

Out of nowhere, another protestor with a bullhorn started screaming, "Impeach him now. Impeach him now. Impeach him now."

The police went to arrest this individual also, and while doing that, two crowds converged. They banded together and started pulling out rotten food from their bags. They proceeded to throw the rotten food at the mayor and said, "Go home, you useless coward and government bureaucrat."

The police went to disperse the crowd and arrested those who threw food at the mayor. Some were arrested, but most of them managed to get away. The mayor was drenched in the foul aroma and putrid stench of rotten food. The rest of the press conference was cancelled, and the mayor was whisked away in a hurry.

CHAPTER 103

It was Monday morning and the beginning of the workweek for Draven. Draven went back to work, while Asia continued the process of making plans for her upcoming trip to Hawaii. Draven wondered what the day would bring him and thought last week was the work experience from hell. He endured two riots and had the only lead as to the identity of the serial killer disintegrate before his very eyes. He thought that it could not get any worse than that, but he would be proven wrong shortly.

Detective Overstreet arrived at the police station and noticed that the other detectives were in a somber mood. They were all present when both riots took place and felt frustrated that the identity of the serial killer had not been ascertained yet. The detectives continued to work around the clock on the case and followed up on leads pertaining to it. Most of the police force was born and raised in San Francisco, and they had deep roots in the city. They loved the diversity and openness of the city and felt that someone was exploiting this to harm other people. They desperately wanted to catch the killer and take that monster off the streets before even more unspeakable harm to the general public took place.

Draven went to go speak to Captain Hammer and noticed that he was on the phone with another person. Captain Hammer just listened, and his only response was, "Yes, sir." He looked sheepish and totally emasculated and dejected. His face was sunk, and he had the look of total shock on it.

Draven asked another detective what was going on, and he said, "Captain Hammer is talking to the mayor, and the mayor is blaming him for the events that took place last week. He is threatening to fire him if the case is not solved soon."

After Draven was done talking to the other detective, Captain Hammer finished his conversation with the mayor and requested that Draven enter his office. Captain Hammer looked disgusted and could barely make eye contact with Draven. He said, "The mayor demanded you completely removed from the case and if you refuse, I was to take your badge and gun away and you were to be placed on paid leave and face a review board based on a charge of insubordination."

Draven could hardly believe what he was hearing and had to sit down. He informed Captain Hammer that he had spent numerous hours on the case and had plans to follow up on other leads pertaining to it. Draven felt that the mayor was blaming him for the fiascos that took place last week and voiced this to Captain Hammer.

Captain Hammer said, "I agree with you, but my hands are tied." He then informed Draven, "Effective immediately, you are off the case," and advised him to stay away from it.

CHAPTER 104

Draven finished his work at the police station and decided to go to his favorite watering hole, EZ5. He wanted to unwind and forget about today's events. It had been a very traumatic day, and Draven needed to put it behind him. He thought that a night at the bar along with one of his closest friends, who happened to be working that day, would do the trick. Draven thought about talking to Asia concerning today's events but decided that she was happy about her upcoming trip and he did not want to ruin it.

Draven ordered his favorite alcoholic beverage, red caramel-flavored Grolsch beer, and proceeded to talk to the bartender. They talked about Bay Area sports, which included the upcoming NFL Draft, and both agreed that the San Francisco 49ers had several glaring holes that they needed to fill before the season started. They also talked about Asia and her upcoming trip to Hawaii and Little Jimmi.

While they were talking, another news report flashed on the television set, and it talked about the Great Bayview explosion along with subsequent fire. The reporter said that the twenty-year-old anniversary of the explosion along with subsequent fire had recently passed and showed photos of the victims. It showed images of the initial damage done by the fire as well as the cleanup that resulted in the rebuilding of the area.

After that, Channel 4 Kron News at ten came on, and the featured story was the serial killer who appeared to be targeting women in San Francisco. The reporter talked about police not being able to find a connection linking the victims together, and Draven was happy that they did not know that the killer selected his victims based on blood type. That revelation might chase him away or cause the killer to be more careful. He needed him to be sloppy and make a mistake so that Draven could catch him.

CHAPTER 105

Asia completed all the tasks pertaining to her upcoming trip to Hawaii in two days. She felt relieved that it was finally over and she could focus all her attention on her upcoming trip without any pending worries. It felt like a whirlwind of responsibility had been lifted and she could let go of it at last. She decided to celebrate this accomplishment by spending the day with Little Jimmi. Her vacation had officially started, and it was the first day of spring. Draven was still at work and would not be home for hours.

Asia decided to take Little Jimmi for a walk at Golden Gate Park. She knew Draven took him there before and he loved it. Little Jimmi loved the fresh air and the feeling of the green, newly grown grass as he rubbed it all over his body. Little Jimmi loved being able to run carefree in the park and play with the other dogs like himself who were gradually progressing through puppyhood at breakneck speed.

While they were at Golden Gate Park, Asia decided to visit the Japanese Tea Garden. She had been there before, and it was an extremely relaxing experience, which she never forgot and it left an indelible mark on her. She loved the flowers and plants that surrounded the Japanese Tea Garden in a majestic tapestry of colors. She enjoyed seeing the brightly colored orange and white Koi and other fish that were in the pond. Asia loved the relaxing atmosphere and the openness of the other patrons in that area who engaged in conversation with one another.

It was a perfect day for a visit to the Japanese Tea Garden. It was a hot, sunny day, and the hummingbirds were spreading their sound of happiness and joy throughout the garden. The raccoons and squirrels were loose, roaming the freshly cut grass. The plants were spreading all their wonderful scents throughout

Golden Gate Park. There was not a cloud in sight, and a slight breeze permeated the air.

After visiting the Japanese Tea Garden, she decided to take Little Jimmi to the outdoor dog park at Golden Gate Park. Little Jimmi was excited and could not contain himself from his inner jubilation. He started jumping up and down at the anticipation of the hours of fun that awaited him. Little Jimmi loved running, especially playing fetch with his favorite orange ball, and this also helped him get a restful sleep at night.

Asia and Little Jimmi played for hours. She threw the ball and watched as Little Jimmi would chase after it. He would then bring it back to her, and the process would repeat itself. She watched as Little Jimmi ran with the other dogs and played with them. He looked so carefree, and Little Jimmi appeared to be having the time of his life. Little Jimmi seemed to be a happy dog and enjoying his progression from puppyhood to adult dog.

They stayed at Golden Gate Park until six thirty. On the way home, Asia decided to take Little Jimmi to Baker Beach to watch the sun go down. He had never experienced this before and thought it would be one that he would never forgot. They watched as the bright-orange- yellowish fireball disappeared behind the clouds slowly and gave way to a dark-grayish appearance that permeated the sky. Both watched as a barge passed through the water as this was happening. The fog proceeded to move in, and with that came the crisp coldness that enveloped the air. After that, they both went back to Draven's apartment.

CHAPTER 106

Draven decided to visit Pit Bull's residence one more time to consult with him about the case. He still believed that the killer worked at the Social Security Administration Building on Kearney Street and was using the archived records at this agency to select his victims. He knew that the killer was targeting women who had blood type AB-. Draven spoke to all the staff members at the Social Security Administration who had this blood type, but nothing panned out.

Draven had done his own research on the prevalence of blood type AB- within the United States and discovered that it was extremely rare. Five percent of the population in the United States had this blood type, and that narrowed down the pool of suspects considerably. He thought that this information would have made it easier to catch the killer and end the nightmare that was plaguing the city, but he was proven wrong. The identity of this killer seemed to be one mystery that he could not solve, and each attempt was leading to more heartache along with dead ends. He was at his wit's end and needed help in this case desperately.

With that, Draven needed to consult with Pit Bull pertaining to the facts of the case and the next course of action to take to solve it. He contacted Pit Bull via telephone and made an arrangement to see him later that day in his residence at one. Draven was aware that although he had been taken off the case, he was risking his career by choosing to continue investigating it and decided that the risk was worth the possible harm that could be done to his career.

Draven arrived at Pit Bull's residence and was buzzed in the door immediately. He proceeded to walk into the living room where Pit Bull was playing pool while watching ESPN as the NBA playoffs were on. Pit Bull seemed to be excited because the Los Angeles Lakers had advanced to the playoffs and they were on a winning streak. They had been a surprise in the sports world because they were not expected to go anywhere this year. The Golden State Warriors had been eliminated from playoff contention, and as a result, Draven had decided to shift his attention to the San Francisco Giants because baseball just started and they showed promise this year.

Pit Bull introduced Draven to Roxanna Ladd. Roxanna Ladd shook Draven's hand before taking a puff from her vape pen and said, "Pleased to meet you."

Pit Bull informed Draven that Roxanna was a tech aficionado who could do anything when it came to technical support and said, "She's here to do a maintenance check on my surveillance equipment. I normally do it myself, but my back is killing me, and I cannot bend over to do that anymore." He also said, "It is safe to talk about the case around Roxanna, and I trust her."

CHAPTER 107

Roxanna listened with rapt attention as Draven and Pit Bull reviewed the facts of the case together. She listened while Draven talked about the steps that he had already taken in his attempt to solve the case. Roxanna could clearly see that Draven cared deeply about the safety of the residents in San Francisco and desperately wanted to solve the case but felt intense frustration because he failed to do this at every turn. She could tell that Draven was open to any suggestion and option pertaining to additional steps that could be taken to meet this goal.

She decided to offer Draven a suggestion and requested additional information pertaining to staff members from the Social Security Administration that were interviewed as possible suspects during the course of the investigation. Draven talked about reviewing all the employee records via the Social Security Administration database. Roxanna inquired as to the accuracy of this database and wondered if it was complete and how often it was updated.

Draven was intrigued by what Roxanna said and requested that she continue. Roxanna informed Draven that some companies farm various tasks that needed to be completed by other agencies. Those employees were listed as permanent employees of the agency that they were contracted from and not the one they were currently working at. In this case, the Social Security Administration could have partnered with another company handling tech support. This employee then could be listed as a permanent employee for the contracting company and possibly never showed up in the employee database for SSA but could be granted access to all the information housed in the database.

Draven's mind was reeling at this sudden development and desperately wanted to speak to Walter Sampson. He wanted to do this immediately but could not continue investigating the SSA because he was taken off the case by his superior and could be arrested for insubordination if the mayor found out he was still investigating it. That could result in a review board permanently stripping Draven of his badge and possible jail time. Draven decided that he covertly needed to continue the investigation and wondered if Roxanna could quietly hack into the SSA employee database to further investigate the individuals who work there.

CHAPTER 108

The killer was home and worried that he might get caught. The police had been at his office twice this week and talked to numerous staff members about the unsolved murders occurring throughout San Francisco. The killer began thinking, *Did I make a mistake, and have I been careless in any way?* He decided some of the trophies he kept from the murdered victims needed to be discarded just in case his house was raided by the police and others hidden away. With that being said, he took mementos of his murdered victims such as T- shirts, jewelry, and other personal properties and placed them in an incinerator and watched them reduced to ashes in a matter of minutes. He took the scrapbook documenting all his killings and news clippings and put it in his secret hiding place.

The killer then proceeded to get ready for tonight's abduction of his latest victim. He had selected his newest victim three weeks ago, and today was the day. The killer was excited, and to him, this was Christmas. He could hardly contain himself. He could hardly wait to hear her scream in agony and beg him to stop. But he thought, *All good things come to those who wait.* With that, he took out his black long-sleeve sweatshirt, ski mask, gloves, pants, jacket, and white handkerchief, which would be dipped in alcohol today. He also got out his night-vision goggles and made sure that they worked. When done, he mumbled to himself, *All set and ready to go.*

CHAPTER 109

Roxanna Ladd proceeded to hack into the Social Security Administration database and was able to break into it within minutes. She was shocked by the weakness of its firewall protection and security program. This agency housed vast amounts of personal information, which included names, addresses, social security numbers, birthdates, and other personal items that could do enormous, untold damage if the wrong person got a hold of it.

Draven directed Roxanna to the file that housed SSA's employment records. Roxanna clicked on this option, and a username and password were requested. She, somehow, was able to bypass this, and within minutes, they had a listing of all the employees who worked for the Social Security Administration in San Francisco. She then sorted this information by location, and within minutes, a listing of all the employees who worked at the Kearney Street Branch appeared on the computer screen. She then selected another option to sort them by blood type, and another list was generated. These were the same people that Draven interviewed earlier, and none of these leads had panned out. "Damn, another dead end," Draven said.

Draven then remembered what Roxanna had said earlier about work being contracted with outside companies. He instructed Roxanna to search if any company was contracted to handle tech support. She began by looking under a file entitled "Auxiliary Operations." Roxanna clicked on this file, and a listing of Genentech Security Systems flashed on the screen.

Draven immediately took out his cell phone at a fever pitch and conducted an online search for Genentech Security Systems. Within seconds, a Web site for Genentech Security Systems appeared on the screen, talking about this company handling tech support for numerous government agencies including the

Social Security Administration. Draven heard his heart race at the thought that this might be the big break that he had been waiting for in the case. He then accessed the employee directory, and a list of individuals who worked for this company flashed on the screen.

Draven relayed this information to Roxanna and could hardly contain himself at the thought of finally identifying the name of the serial killer He then had Roxanna hack into the employee records for Genentech Security Systems. Draven informed Roxanna that he was looking for a man with a blood type AB- and explained to her that it was an extremely rare one. Roxanna then proceeded to hack into the Genentech Security System Web site and entered the human resources portal. Again, a username and password were requested. She again bypassed this system, and in no time, the option to view the employee files was on the screen. They were sorted by blood type, and Draven watched the computer process this request. It was a frantic, anxiety-ridden wait of five minutes, but finally, the request was granted, and the computer spit out a name. It read William Harcourt, and he was the only one who worked for Genentech Security Systems who had this blood type. Draven jumped out of his seat with excitement and relief because he knew that they had finally found his man. The man who terrorized San Francisco for nine long months had finally been identified, and it was now time to bring this monster to justice.

CHAPTER 110

Asia dropped off Little Jimmi to Draven's neighbor and proceeded to drive herself home. She was excited about her upcoming trip to Hawaii tomorrow morning and needed to complete some last-minute packing. Her flight was scheduled to depart at twelve, but Asia wanted to give the baggage handlers plenty of time to perform all safety protocols, which could take time, so she requested for an Uber ride to come get her at nine. She wanted to leave nothing to chance. She knew that since September 11, 2001, security had been tight at the airport, especially when it came to luggage allowed on the plane.

Asia pulled into her driveway and proceeded to open the garage door. She then drove her car inside and could hardly wait to complete her last-minute packing. Asia thought she was done packing but remembered some items she wanted to bring to her trip. After packing, she planned to take a warm, soothing bath and go to bed because she had a big day tomorrow morning.

Asia parked her car in the garage and exited it. She was getting ready to use the remote control to close the garage door when she suddenly heard a loud crash. When looking up, she saw a figure completely clad in black standing in front of her. She knew right away that this was the serial killer targeting women in San Francisco and realized her very survival depended on what actions she took within the next several seconds. Asia got ready to defend herself, but before she could do anything, she felt an excruciating, burning sensation in her eyes and could not see anything. The killer had pepper-sprayed her eyes and, while she was distracted by the pain, placed a white handkerchief completely soaked in alcohol around her mouth.

Asia passed out instantly and was placed into the killer's van. He closed the garage door so as not to attract any attention from the neighbors and those passing by and drove off with Asia at the back of the van. Nobody heard anything, and another victim had been taken.

CHAPTER 111

Pit Bull, Roxanna, and Draven continued the online research pertaining to the background of Mr. William Harcourt. They discovered, upon further research, that Mr. Harcourt had been employed by Genentech Security Systems for the past ten years and moved from Phoenix to San Francisco twenty years ago. Draven noted that his arrival date in San Francisco coincided with the day of the explosion along with the Great Bayview Fire in San Francisco. They learned that Mr. Harcourt resided at 33 Evans Street and did not have any children and was single. Draven also noted that Mr. Harcourt resided in the area that had been rebuilt after the explosion and subsequent fire that took place in San Francisco twenty years ago.

Draven noticed that the suspected killer had two connections to the Great Bayview explosion along with subsequent fire. He thought that this could not be a coincidence and pondered to himself, *I bet that he has an entire blood-draining laboratory set up in his residence, and he probably converted it from an abandoned, old, underground, meth lab.* Draven knew from past experiences that some drug labs were located underground and that residences in San Francisco had fallout shelters connected to vast underground networks of tunnels constructed prior to the Y2K scare in 2000, where people thought the whole country would shut down and be plunged into an economic nightmare. It did not happen, but that caused individuals to construct underground bunkers and a vast network of tunnels as a buffer against that possible disaster.

CHAPTER 112

After conducting the research pertaining to Mr. William Harcourt, Draven was faced with a dilemma. He obtained enough background information about Mr. William Harcourt to realize and draw a firm conclusion that he was the serial killer he had been searching for all this time. His long, exhaustive investigation had finally paid off. Mr. William Harcourt possessed all the intangibles that led Draven to this conclusion, which included blood type, occupation, and other vital pieces of information. But on the other hand, this information was obtained via questionable and borderline, illegal methods. He could be brought before a review board and stripped of his detective shield and face jail time if this ever came out.

Draven reminded himself that the risk was worth it. He could not let this monster roam the streets and continue to target innocent victims and needed to relay this information to the individuals who could act on it. Draven wanted vengeance for all those innocent women who had been killed and tortured by this maniac. They demanded justice, and Draven desperately wanted to give it to them. He had never yearned for something this deep and strong while working a case. Draven knew that his conscience would not rest until this monster was taken off the streets and silenced forever.

He thought long and hard about it and finally reached a solution to this presenting problem. Draven decided to have Roxanna contact the tip line at the San Francisco Police Department via telephone and relay this information to the officer handling it. They would have to act on it due to the negative press that the case was generating from the media along with the general public and verify this information. Draven thought it was a great idea and watched as Roxanna contacted the San Francisco Police Department.

Draven thought that as a possible longshot, he could be placed back on the case. He was the original detective handling the case and knew everything about it. Draven thought it better he be placed back on the case rather than have to bring another detective up to date on the details surrounding it.

CHAPTER 113

Draven headed back to the police station, and immediately, Captain Hammer pulled him into his office. Captain Hammer informed Draven that he was being placed back on the case and told him to follow up on a huge lead received from an anonymous source on the tip line earlier this morning. Draven was extremely excited and eager to follow up on this lead and catch this monster plaguing the streets of San Francisco. Before leaving Captain Hammer's Office, Draven inquired about the mayor's response to him being reassigned to the case. Captain Hammer said, "Let me deal with that. He will never be a problem again."

Before leaving the captain's office, he said, "I am going to see the Honorable Oliver Wendell Whitehurst in order to obtain a search warrant for Mr. Harcourt's residence and place of employment." Captain Hammer thanked Draven for keeping him updated on the steps he was taking to solve the case. Draven informed Captain Hammer that he had obtained this information before being taken off the case.

Draven exited the captain's office, and he was completely shocked by the change in the captain's attitude and demeanor. The captain wanted the case solved and was not going to allow politicians or a local government bureaucracy stand in his way. He was prepared to take all the steps necessary to catch the killer and close the case.

Draven went to see the Honorable Oliver Wendell Whitehurst at his office and noticed that virtually nothing had changed in it since their previous meeting. He did see that an autographed picture of Sen. Bernie Sanders from Vermont was on his wall. They exchanged pleasantries, and Draven informed him, "I'm here to obtain a search warrant for Mr. William Harcourt's residence and place of employment. He was the chief suspect in an ongoing murder investigation pertaining to the serial killer plaguing the city." He also presented other details regarding the case in his ongoing effort to obtain a search warrant.

The judge decided to grant Draven the search warrant. Draven was shocked that it was granted and processed right away. Draven knew that the judge wanted this killer off the streets of San Francisco as badly as he did and was prepared to do whatever it took to achieve this goal. Once the search warrant had been signed, the judge presented it to Draven, and he thanked the judge for his assistance. He then proceeded to head back to the police station to meet with the task force and formulate a plan to execute it.

CHAPTER 114

Draven went back to the police station, and everyone was excited to have him reinstated onto the task force created to catch the serial killer plaguing San Francisco. They hugged Draven and welcomed him back. Detective Overstreet was happy to be back on the task force, and his first order of business was to inform the other members that he obtained the identity of the man suspected to be the serial killer. He gave them the name of the killer and presented his home address, occupation, and place of employment.

The task force was in a state of shock and wanted to move on this information as quickly as possible. Draven informed them of the search warrant he obtained from the Honorable Oliver Wendell Whitehurst earlier today for the suspect's residence and place of employment, which was the Social Security Administration on Kearney Street but had been contracted by Genentech Security Systems to handle SSA's tech support. Draven informed the rest of the task force that he wanted to hit the suspect's place of employment first.

Numerous members of the task force were astonished by this development and revelation. They could not believe that the killer worked at the Social Security Administration on Kearney Street and was right under their noses this whole time. Some members of the task force talked about going to this facility on numerous occasions to take care of personal business and thought that the killer probably walked right by this individual at times. They thought about the killer having access to all personal information, and it disgusted them. Draven also talked about SSA's supervisor, Mr. Walter Sampson, being extremely cooperative throughout the investigation and assured them that this individual would not be a problem when they execute the search warrant.

CHAPTER 115

Draven and the rest of the task force continued to meet in the conference room well into the evening. Lunch was ordered at twelve so workers would not pass out due to hunger and a sharp, dangerous drop in blood sugar levels. During the meeting, Draven flashed a diagram pertaining to the layout of the Social Security Administration Building on Kearney Street. He informed them that their initial point of contact would be the security guard who was stationed at the front entrance. This individual would escort the task force to Mr. Walter Sampson's office, whom they would present the search warrant to so he could direct them to the area where Mr. William Harcourt worked. He informed everyone that the layout of the building was confusing and reminded people to stick together. Draven said, "We do not want anyone getting lost because the success of the mission depends on the search warrant being executed efficiently and professionally."

Draven continued with his briefing and plan formulation pertaining to the execution of the search warrant. "If Mr. Harcourt is at his desk," Draven instructed, "he is to be immediately detained for questioning." Draven added, "His computer and paper files are to be seized as evidence, which includes all information stored in them." Draven went on to say, "That should give us enough evidence to arrest and charge Mr. William Harcourt with eight counts of first-degree, premeditated murder. That should put him away for a long time and keep our streets safe again."

CHAPTER 116

Draven started talking about his plans to execute the search warrant at the suspect's place of residence. Detective Overstreet informed the task force that this was to be done immediately if the suspect was not at work. He told the task force that he wanted it done this way to ensure that the suspect would not slip through their fingers and get away.

Draven then brought out a diagram of the suspect's residence. He proceeded to review it with them in great detail. Draven informed the task force assembled in the conference room that the suspect lived in a one-story house with a garage and basement at the back. He said that the basement possibly housed an elaborate, homemade, blood- draining machine with a vast network of underground tunnels connected to it.

Draven informed the task force that he would go through the front door of the suspect's house with a small contingent to issue the search warrant to him. One contingent of the SWAT team would come in through the front window. Another one would come in through the enclosure on the roof. A second wave would surround the garage to ensure that the suspect does not try to escape. The last group would proceed through the basement. Draven reminded them to be careful when coming in through the basement. The layout pertaining to that area of the residence was unclear, and changes could have been made to it.

CHAPTER 117

Detective Overstreet and the task force went to the Social Security Administration on Kearney Street eager to dispense justice and put the nightmare plaguing San Francisco to an end. It was a warm, beautiful morning, and the sun silhouetted across the sky. The hummingbirds were singing, and their songs illuminated the air. The traffic was light, and the scene was finally set to dispense justice for all those women who lost their lives to this madman.

Draven and the task force approached the building on Kearney Street with determination and vigor. They were immediately greeted by a security guard when they entered the building. Draven flashed his badge and presented the search warrant to the security guard and requested that the task force, assembled in the building, be escorted to Walter Sampson's office.

The security guard proceeded to escort Draven and the rest of the task force to Walter Sampson's Office. When they arrived at his office, Mr. Sampson was waiting for them outside. He had a stern look on his face, and Mr. Sampson's shirt sleeves were rolled up. He talked about being eager to continue cooperating with the police in whatever capacity was needed to put an end to the nightmare that engulfed San Francisco and seemed to have no finality.

Draven presented the search warrant to Mr. Sampson and watched as he reviewed it intensely. Mr. Sampson was in a state of shock after reading it and could not believe Mr. William Harcourt was the prime suspect in the unsolved murders plaguing San Francisco. He said that this individual was his best worker and never created problems for him. He was a quiet man who mainly kept to himself and was pleasant to everyone around him.

Mr. Sampson felt that he needed to sit down because of the recent news and thought it had to be a huge mistake. He said to himself, "Maybe, upon further investigation, they will discover that he is not the killer and this has been a horrible mistake." He just could not picture Mr. William Harcourt as a cold-blooded killer and felt that if it was him, he had been duped by a brilliant sociopath who has a PhD in manipulating other people around him and projecting a false image of himself to the world.

Mr. Sampson proceeded to escort the task force to Mr. Harcourt's Office. Upon arrival at Mr. Harcourt's office, they immediately took possession of his computer and made arrangements for the forensics team to begin conducting a thorough search of all the files in it. They obtained a master key for the file cabinet in Mr. Harcourt's office and had Mr. Sampson open it so the contents could immediately be examined by the task force. Yellow tape was placed across the door of Mr. Harcourt's office to seal off the room from the press, onlookers, and other people. A police officer was placed in front of the door to stand guard and keep all non-police personnel away from the room while the search was taking place. The other detectives continued searching the office for any valuable evidence that could confirm Mr. Harcourt was the killer.

The forensics team started to analyze the files and other information that was stored in the computer. They were able to bypass the firewall protection and access the main database of the Social Security Administration. They went through his browsing history and hit *paydirt*. Mr. Harcourt had saved all the Social Security card replacement applications for each victim, and upon further investigation, they found a file he created with all these documents on them. In reviewing the applications, the detectives discovered that each one had the applicant's blood type and home address. When looking at the blood types, they found out that the applicants had blood type AB-. But one applicant stood out, and it was a recent one, no more than two days ago, and Draven needed to be alerted about this immediately.

CHAPTER 118

Asia woke up from her slumber in a pitch-black room. She could not see anything, and for a moment, Asia forgot where she was. Then Asia remembered getting out of her car in the garage and being attacked by a figure clad entirely in black who left her unconscious. The rest was a blur. She did not get a good look at her assailant but knew it was probably the serial killer plaguing the city and attacking those poor, innocent women. She figured that it was the same person who left her tied up and confined in this room.

Asia was scared and frightened inside, but she knew that remaining calm was her only chance of survival. The killer would feed off her panic if she chose to show it, and so she decided to shut down her emotions and use stone-cold logic to increase her chance of surviving this ordeal.

Asia was in the room for a long time, and it felt like an eternity. She was engulfed in total darkness while confined in that room and utilized different mental exercises to maintain her sanity. She thought of Draven and figured that he was marshaling the entire San Francisco Police Force to rescue her. Asia knew that Draven would never rest until she was safe, and that gave her solace along with inner peace.

Asia attempted to move her arms and legs but was unable to do this. She figured that her arms and legs were tied to something, and this made movement impossible. She attempted to do the same with her head and feet, but she was met with similar results. Asia drew the same conclusion, and her thoughts drifted back again to Draven. Asia once again thought about Draven coming to rescue her, and this placed her anxiety at ease.

CHAPTER 119

One of the forensic team members called Det. Overstreet over and wanted to talk to him about the files that were stored in Mr. Harcourt's computer. Upon reviewing the applications for replacement Social Security cards that Mr. Harcourt had downloaded and saved on his computer, the forensic team noticed that the last entry was incredibly alarming and Draven needed to be made aware of this. It hit close to home and concerned someone he was romantically involved with. It was an open secret at the San Francisco Police Station that Draven and Asia were an item. It could not be hidden or kept quiet no matter how hard they tried.

Draven came over immediately and spoke to one of the forensic technicians. This individual informed Det. Overstreet that Mr. William Harcourt is the serial killer and there were plenty of evidence on the suspect's computer to confirm this. Draven was ecstatic about this revelation and eager to execute the search warrant on the suspect's residence. He had a strong feeling that the killer was currently at his residence and, more than likely, in the process of taking another innocent, poor soul from this world. He wanted to execute the search warrant right now and thought that local government, bureaucratic, red tape would make this impossible, but Draven would soon find out how wrong he was.

The forensic team member requested that Draven sit down because another revelation came to light during the investigation of Mr. Harcourt's files. He informed Draven that the killer had downloaded a recently completed application for a replacement Social Security card, and it was for Asia Francisco. It was dated two days ago, and her blood type was listed as AB-. He went on to say, "We have attempted to contact her already via cell phone and have not received an answer. It keeps ringing and ringing."

Detective Overstreet sprang into action. He halted the investigation and called an impromptu meeting in Mr. Harcourt's office. He advised one of the officers to close the door so the press and anyone outside the office would not get word of what he was about to tell them. He informed all the police personnel gathered in the room that Asia Francisco possibly had been kidnapped by the serial killer. He went on to say, "We need to act immediately because her life is in danger, and her very survival depends on the actions that we take right now."

CHAPTER 120

Draven and the task force decided that the search warrant for the suspect's residence needed to be executed immediately. Asia's life was at stake and moments wasted were the difference between life along with death for her. Draven knew that Mr. William Harcourt was a cold-blooded, vicious killer who did not have any remorse for anyone and would not hesitate to take Asia's life. To him, this was a game where the only losers were Asia and Draven. Draven also knew that the other detectives loved Asia and deeply cared about her and would not hesitate to protect her from bodily harm even at the risk of their own lives.

Draven and the task force reviewed the plan that they formed earlier. They made some last-minute changes to it because of the urgency of the situation that lay before them. After this was done, Draven reminded them that this needed to be executed proficiently, efficiently, and quickly. Draven informed the task force assembled in the room that the killer was a brilliant, calculating man, who escaped police detection for a long time by being smart and cunning, covering his tracks, and leaving an escape plan if he was in danger of being caught. He informed them that the killer probably installed safeguards in his home and was prepared for any unexpected along with unwanted visitors.

Captain Hammer was present during the briefing and decided that he would be going with Draven and the other police personnel gathered in the room to assist them with executing the search warrant at the suspect's residence later that day. He loved Asia too and thought of her as a big sister whom he was extremely protective of. Captain Hammer would not let anyone harm Asia and, if needed, defend Asia against any possible threats to her personal safety with his very life without a moment's hesitation. He also wanted to see the expression on this monster's face when he was finally caught and forced to answer for his crimes along with the harm that he caused other people. To Captain Hammer, that was true justice, and he wanted to be one of the instruments that would dispense it.

CHAPTER 121

Draven and the task force sprang into action after the plan to execute the search warrant at the suspect's residence had been finalized. Draven and Captain Hammer went into Draven's car and proceeded to drive to the suspect's residence. They drove to the suspect's house at a frantic pace and mind-blowing sense of urgency. The other detectives and the rest of the task force followed behind. Draven advised the police officers to keep their sirens and lights off so as not to alert the suspect that they had arrived at his house. They wanted to maintain an element of surprise, and Draven knew full well that Asia's fate hinged on this.

Draven contacted the commander of the SWAT team via telephone before leaving with the rest of the task force to go to the suspect's residence. He told this individual that he would be informing the SWAT team of their role in assisting with the execution of the search warrant once arriving at the suspect's residence. He presented the commander of the SWAT team with the suspect's address and informed him that he and the rest of the task force would be there in twenty minutes. He also told the commander that the suspect had kidnapped Asia and that, more than likely, she was in the residence being held against her will. The commander said, "I will advise my team to exercise extreme caution when going into the suspect's residence so she is not placed in greater danger." Draven thanked him for his understanding.

They arrived at the suspect's residence and waited for the SWAT team. The residence had the look of a classic, old Victorian home that had been manicured and well maintained. The grass was dark green and recently cut and shaped to perfection as if a professional had been taking care of it for years. The house was surrounded by a lush, vibrant garden that was filled with a variety of plants. The bees and other insects were playing in the garden and spreading nectar to all the surrounding foliage, ensuring continued growth in the years to come. A candy apple-red Ford Mustang stood parked in the driveway, and the sun bounced off the car as if it had been recently polished and was ready for a night of unrivaled excitement on the town.

Detective Overstreet could not believe that a vicious, cold-blooded, cunning monster could live at this residence. The house was stunningly beautiful and gorgeous, and the owner had done a masterful touch when decorating the residence. It was filled with statues and other decorations, which added luster to it. It was clear the owner had pride pertaining to ownership of the property. It was also clear to Draven that behind this home stood a chamber of horrors where unimaginable evil had taken place. Before storming the residence, Draven decided that the task force and SWAT team needed to have a meeting in the park located near the suspect's residence.

CHAPTER 122

Draven and the task force parked their cars in a wooded, secluded part of the park near Mr. Harcourt's residence. The task force and SWAT team proceeded to move in a deliberate, methodical manner so as not to make noise and to attract attention. They wanted to maintain an element of surprise to ensure that they apprehended the suspect and finally brought him to justice. They all knew that any loud, startling noises and sounds could derail their plans and place everyone in danger.

Upon arriving at the scene, Draven introduced himself to the commander of the SWAT team. He said. "My name is Det. Overstreet, and I am pleased to meet you. Today is the day."

The Commander responded by saying, "I am Comd. Murphy, and my team is ready to go. Awaiting your orders."

Draven proceeded to introduce himself to the rest of the SWAT team. They were all young and appeared to be in great physical shape. He could tell that they maintained a healthy diet and exercised on a regular basis. They all looked and acted like professionals, which Draven admired. These individuals seemed to be eager to put an end to this monster's carnage once and for all. They also voiced extreme concern about Asia's safety because she was trapped inside with this monster and the killer had cruel intentions in his heart toward Asia.

Draven then introduced the SWAT team to each member of the task force. He watched as they shook hands and met each other for the first time. When done, he informed the task force and SWAT team that a meeting would take place shortly in the area of the park designated for picnics and camping pertaining to storming the suspect's residence.

The task force and SWAT team reconvened several minutes later. The immediate area was heavily wooded and surrounded by huge, mighty oak trees that engulfed the area and provided camouflage. This ensured that the task force and SWAT team maintained invisibly if the suspect was to look out his window at the surrounding area.

The area where the meeting was conducted served as a camping and picnic site. It had tables and benches for socializing with others and eating food. The area contained a barbeque pit for cooking food. Draven located one of the tables and placed a huge paper diagram on it of the suspect's residence. He brought a small portable lamp from his car and placed batteries in it. The lamp was turned on, and the light illuminated the diagram of the suspect's residence for all to see. Draven then adjusted the intensity of the light to make sure it was not visible beyond the park for the killer to see outside his window.

Draven informed the commander and the rest of the SWAT team and the task force that the meeting was going to start. He began outlining the steps that the task force would take pertaining to executing the search warrant at the suspect's residence and rescuing Asia from possible harm. Draven said, "I, the captain, and a small contingent of police officers will attempt to issue the search warrant at the front door of the residence. Another contingent composed of two detectives and police officers will approach the residence from the backdoor and, when given the signal, blow it open." Draven continued on. "The SWAT team will have two units enter the home. One will come in through the front windows and another one via the enclosure on the roof. Another contingent of police officers will come in through the main tunnel that connects it to the basement and leads to the blood-draining lab. This will ensure that the suspect does not escape." Draven added, "Asia is more than likely being held captive in the blood-draining lab and probably feels weak from malnourishment and suffered from unspeakable trauma while trapped in that house with the killer. So please be careful when discharging firearms because her reflexes and reaction time might be impaired. We do not want her hit in the crossfire." After the meeting was over, the task force along with SWAT team dispersed and went about making preparations to handle the business at hand.

Everyone proceeded to get into position for the upcoming raid on the suspect's residence. Draven, Captain Hammer, and a small contingent of police officers approached the front door. Weapons were drawn, and Draven had the search warrant in his hands, ready to be served to an unsuspecting William Harcourt. One unit of the SWAT team led by Comd. Murphy ascended up the front of the house via steel cables and made arrangements to crash through the front windows when the signal came. As part of the preparation, they made sure that their guns were loaded and bulletproof shields ready to be employed when needed. Another unit started climbing up the roof slowly but carefully via steel cables so as to not to make a sound and alert the suspect that they would be coming in through an enclosure in it. A third unit composed of two detectives and several police officers approached the rear of the house near the garage and placed plastic explosives on the backdoor in preparation to blow it when the signal came. The last unit consisting of three detectives and police officers went through the main tunnel in the basement and made it to the door that housed the blood-draining lab. Firearms were out, and everyone awaited Draven's instructions. This whole operation was done in total silence, and everyone awaited eagerly to storm the suspect's residence.

While the contingent of detectives and police officers stationed at the backdoor near the garage awaited Draven's orders, they heard incoherent, garbled sounds coming from the radios attached to their belts. It was Draven, and he had altered part of the plan pertaining to the unit that was stationed in the backdoor near the garage. He talked about consulting the diagram further pertaining to the suspect's residence and discovering that a fuse box that provided electricity for the house was located near the backdoor of the garage. Draven instructed one member of this unit to locate it and told him to cut the power the moment that they blew the backdoor open. Draven said, "This would completely confuse the killer and more than likely cause him to panic. They could then go in and arrest him."

He listened as the detectives responded by saying, "Okay and got it."

The only commotion came from the sounds of a struggle that was taking place in the blood-draining lab. The contingent of detectives and police officers gathered outside the door of the blood-draining lab could hear it clearly and were concerned about Asia's safety. They could hear Asia screaming frantically as she fought off the numerous advances of the killer. The detectives and police officers could tell that Asia was in serious danger and waited anxiously for Draven to give the order to begin storming the residence. The wait seemed like an eternity, and their concerns about Asia's safety worsened as each moment passed.

CHAPTER 123

Asia was passed out when the killer arrived in the room. He had given her a powerful sedative earlier in the day, and it caused Asia to fall into a deep, relaxing sleep. While Asia slept, she dreamed that Draven came to rescue and take her away from this hellhole of a prison. When she awoke from her slumber, the killer pressed a button on the remote control he was carrying, and the lights came on, illuminating the room. The room was filled with numerous electrical equipment and monitors, which elicited subtle but continuous buzzing and humming. Besides electrical equipment, the room had various tubes that lined the walls and a small door on the right side that the killer used to enter and exit.

The killer wore a light-blue surgical gown that covered his entire body. He was a small but well-proportioned male who gave the impression that he took care of himself and maintained a healthy diet. Beyond that, she could not provide anyone with more details pertaining to the killer's physical description. Asia attempted to look at the killer's face but noticed that it was covered up completely with a surgical headdress and mask and googles that the killer used to maintain visibility.

The killer spoke to Asia and told her to remain calm. He proceeded to try to give her a sedative, but Asia began to move her body so as to resist his efforts to inject her with it. The killer then said, "Remain still, and all will be over soon."

Asia started screaming and told him, "Leave me alone, you monster." Sweat was profusely pouring down her face, and Asia's heart started to beat rapidly as if it was coming out of her chest. She continued resisting him with all her force, causing one of the restraints to break, and her left arm was released from it. She then punched the killer in the face, and he fell and banged his head against the hard, cold, unforgiving concrete.

The killer grabbed the back of his head and proceeded to get up off the ground. He checked his left hand and noticed that there was a large amount of blood on it. He said, "You are going to pay dearly for this," and proceeded to approach Asia in an aggressive and threatening manner. Asia was worried because most of her body was still strapped to the metal slab, and this left her unable to fight back from the killer's advances.

CHAPTER 124

The order finally came from Draven, and the siege against the suspect's residence started. Draven knocked on the door and said, "Open up! This is Det. Draven Overstreet from the San Francisco Police Department, and I have a warrant to search this residence." He stepped off to the side of the door while doing this so he could protect himself from any possible incoming gunfire from the suspect. Draven did not receive a response and instructed one of the police officers to use the battering ram to break open the door. The police officer swung the battering ram toward the front door of the residence, and upon impact, it instantly shattered and disintegrated into various fragments that littered the floor. Draven and his small contingent proceeded to enter the residence in a slow and cautious manner, careful to preserve any possible evidence. They conducted a thorough but quick search of the area and discovered that no suspects were present in this section of the house. Draven then took out his portable walkie-talkie and informed the rest of the team that this part of this house was all clear of all suspects.

Commander Murphy and one contingent of the SWAT team burst through the front windows. The front windows instantly shattered and made a loud, piercing sound that echoed throughout the living room of the residence. Shards of glass littered the floor, and the SWAT team could hear their feet crackle as they walked across it. They slowly went through the living room looking for the suspect and any possible signs of Asia Francisco. When done, Comd. Murphy said, "All clear," on his walkie-talkie, which signaled to the rest of the task force that no one was present in that area of the residence.

The second unit of the SWAT team lowered themselves down from the enclosure located on the roof and reached the bottom in moments. They quickly raised their guns while unhooking themselves from the steel cables that they descended from. They made a quick but methodical scan of the area and noticed that they were in a hallway with two doors off to the side. The SWAT team remembered the briefing that Draven gave them earlier pertaining to the layout of the residence and recalled that one door led to a bedroom while another to a bathroom. One member of the SWAT team kicked the door open, and the others charged the bedroom to do a fast but thorough search of it. They did the same with the bathroom and discovered that no one was in either room. When done, one member of the SWAT team got on the walkie-talkie and said, "All clear."

The third unit detonated the plastic explosive, and within seconds, the backdoor blew open. It made a loud, thunderous crash, which reverberated throughout this section of the house. Simultaneously, one member of this team cut the power, and the house was plunged into total, absolute darkness. Before entering this section of the house, the detectives and contingent of police officers put their night-vision goggles on to increase along with improve visibility.

They proceeded to enter the residence and immediately noticed that they were in the den. Their weapons were drawn, and they were ready for any possible contingency that presented itself. The detectives and police officers scanned the area for any fast, sudden movements and individuals present in the room. They noticed that the room was surrounded by bookshelves that contained books and other personal items. They continued searching the room and saw that besides books, this section of the room contained a large collection and assortment of stuffed animals, which signaled, to them, that the suspect was a taxidermist. When done completely scanning the room for any possible suspects and discovering none, one of the detectives pulled out his walkie-talkie and said, "All clear."

The last unit stationed themselves off to the side of the door that led to the blood-draining lab. They swung the battering ram toward the door, and upon contact, the impact blew it off the hingers. The police proceeded to enter the lab and noticed that it had been plunged into total darkness due to the power being cut. They had their guns drawn and night-vision goggles on. They could hear someone screaming and begging the police officers not to shoot. It was Asia Francisco, and she was lying on the floor completely scared and petrified. She was heavily bruised and in desperate need of medical attention.

During the siege of the house, the killer had heard all the commotion and made his escape in the ensuing panic. He grabbed a gun and his night-vision goggles and exited the blood-draining lab through a secret panel off to the side of it. Before doing that, he was able to quickly review the security monitors in the lab scattered throughout the inside and outside of his residence, alerting him that police were storming his home. Besides the security monitors, the killer had a loud, piercing alarm set-up at the lab to inform him of any intruders trying to break into his residence. It went off, and the sound was deafening. The security system was connected to a backup generator, which the killer operated by remote controller, protecting him from any sudden, unexpected power outages.

CHAPTER 125

Detective Overstreet heard one of the detectives say via walkie-talkie, "We have Asia, and she is okay. She is going to be transported immediately to San Francisco General Hospital for a thorough physical examination." He was relieved and immediately went to see Asia, who was still at the blood-draining lab waiting for the ambulance to transport her to San Francisco General Hospital. When Draven arrived at the lab, he could see the police officers and members of the SWAT team trying to soothe Asia due to her being traumatized by this recent experience with the killer. They kept telling Asia that she was safe and nobody would harm her anymore. She wanted to believe them but was still deeply upset by what recently transpired. He went immediately to see Asia, who started crying the instant Draven put his arms around her. This incident had scared Asia, and her initial thought was that she would never see Draven again.

When Asia calmed down and stopped crying, she told Draven that the killer disappeared behind a hidden doorway near the entrance to the lab. Draven and the other police personnel in the lab began a frantic but thorough search of the area for this hidden doorway. Before doing this, they turned the power back on, and the light illuminated the blood-draining lab. The police officers and SWAT team members frantically started touching and feeling the walls for any signs of a hidden entranceway. They needed to apprehend the killer soon; otherwise, this maniac would disappear and, more than likely, never be seen again. He would simply vanish into the outside world and be another name on the streets.

CHAPTER 126

The killer frantically ran through the tunnel at a fever pitch, desperate to reach the other end of it. He had his car parked next to the door, which served as an exit to the tunnel. The killer figured that once he exited the tunnel and managed to get into his car, he could drive off into the sunset, never to be seen again. The killer thought that his plan was foolproof and salvation and freedom laid just beyond that door.

The killer had taken precautions to keep himself hidden and safe if he was ever in danger of being apprehended by law enforcement. He had secured the services of an individual who specialized in creating fraudulent documents, which included identification cards, Social Security numbers, and birth certificates. The killer had paid this individual handsomely for creating these documents and, when picking them up earlier in the week, was impressed by his quality of work and professionalism. He had everything ready on time and did quality work. The killer would definitely utilize his services in the future if they were ever needed again.

The killer continued on his journey toward the end of the tunnel. Sweat profusely poured down his face, and his heart beat rapidly as he progressed through the tunnel. His legs started aching each time his foot pounded the pavement, and more than once, the killer thought about wanting to pass out due to the tremendous amount of energy that he was exerting in an attempt to reach his destination. He thought about giving up and surrendering to the police but did not relish the idea of serving a life sentence at Folsom State Prison. The possibility of the death penalty was not a pleasant thought either. With renewed vigor and determination, the killer continued on his journey.

CHAPTER 127

The SWAT team and the rest of the task force finally located the hidden passageway in the blood-draining lab, which took fifteen minutes of pure agony. Draven thought that they would never discover the hidden passageway. The button to open it was strategically camouflaged against the wall, and this made it difficult, if downright impossible, to locate. It was by chance that Draven and the task force had discovered the button that was used to open the hidden passageway, and they were relieved to do so.

Draven charged through the hidden passageway ahead of the SWAT team and the task force at breakneck speed. He desperately wanted to apprehend the killer and thought if he waited for the SWAT team and the task force to go with him, the suspect would get away. He entered the hidden passageway, and the room was engulfed in total darkness. Draven placed his hands in front of him to begin gathering information about the layout of the room. He could hear himself breathing heavier than usual because he did not know the location of the killer. He said to himself, "The killer could be right at my back, and I would not know it."

Sweat was pouring profusely down his face, and his heart rate was elevated. Draven felt the adrenaline surging throughout his body, and he started subconsciously doing stress reduction exercises to stay in the moment and not panic at the uncertainty around him. He continued feeling his surroundings with his hands. His hands eventually felt the hard, cold, concrete on both sides, and he gathered that these were the walls of the tunnel the killer was in. Draven could feel a slight breeze going up his spine coming from the passageway where he entered the tunnel earlier. Draven continued to pay attention to the sounds around him, hoping that a slight, indiscreet one would give away the location of the killer and put an end to this madness.

CHAPTER 128

Some of the police officers went to examine the security monitors located in the blood-draining lab and noticed that one of them showed Draven in a long, dark tunnel with the killer. They could tell that Draven was unaware that the killer was standing right in front of him. They noticed that the killer was about to aim his gun at Draven's head and shoot him at point-blank range in the face. The police officers, the SWAT team, and other detectives did not have a way of warning Draven about the impending threat to his safety. This could prove fatal to him.

Their chance of ensuring Draven's safety rested in turning the lights in the tunnel back on. One of the police officers looked at the security monitors stationed at the backdoor next to the fuse box and saw that no one was present at this location. He had minutes to spare. The fuse box had a button next to it, which turned the lights on in the tunnel, and he needed to hit this button himself. He began running in a frantic, desperate manner because the police officer knew that Draven's life depended and hinged on it. He started running to this location, and each step was pure agony. He finally arrived at the fuse box and hit the button, which instantly illuminated the tunnel that Drave was walking in.

Draven heard the faint click of a gun while he was in the tunnel and decided to point his gun straight ahead. Suddenly, the lights flew on, and a figure stood in front of Draven with a gun pointed directly at his head. The hammer was cocked, and Draven had seconds to spare. The light momentarily blinded the killer due to the sharp glare in his eyes from the night-vision goggles, so Draven was able to open fire.

The bullets immediately ripped through the killer's lungs and neck. The killer struggled to breathe and felt the blood suffocating his lungs. It poured out of his mouth as he collapsed on the hard, cold, unforgiving pavement, and he felt his life drift away as he breathed his last breath. Draven kicked the gun away from the suspect's hand and saw that the killer's eyes remained wide open in shock and astonishment at what recently transpired. The killer showed no signs of life, and the madness was finally over. The city could sleep in somber rest, knowing that it was safe once again.

CHAPTER 129

The task force and the SWAT team watched the events on one of the security monitors as they unfolded with rapt attention. They saw as Draven pulled the trigger and emptied his clip into the killer. They watched as the bullets penetrated the killer's neck and lungs and he fell to the ground, struggling to breathe. They watched the life drain from his body and saw it reduced to a lifeless corpse incapable of hurting another soul ever again. They cheered as this happened and knew the city would finally have that peaceful, calm sleep because this madman was finally erased from existence.

One of the detectives went to see Asia who was being loaded into the ambulance, and he relayed the good news to her. She was relieved that Draven was safe and wanted to see him immediately. Asia worried the entire time that Draven was trapped with that madman in the tunnel and thought that this would be the last time she saw Draven alive again. She desperately wanted that life she had this past week with Draven and Little Jimmi never to end.

The EMT worker wanted Asia to relax and reminded her that she needed to be transported to San Francisco General Hospital for a thorough medical examination due to recent events. Asia agreed, and they began their journey to the hospital. The EMT worker was extremely gentle and took extra care of her throughout the drive. Asia asked the EMT worker for her name, and she said, "Serena." Asia complimented the EMT worker about the tattoo on her arm and talked about wanting to get another one. Asia thanked her for everything and talked about having the feeling that she was a kind, gentle person, who was a guardian angel for others because she took care of people who were in severe pain and made them feel better.

She requested the name of Serena's assistant, and he said, "Tom." She relayed the same message to him, and they continued on their journey in total relaxation to San Francisco General Hospital without a care in the world.

CHAPTER 130

The coroner came and proceeded to wrap the dead body. Before doing that, he attempted to take its pulse and noticed that the body had none. He pronounced it dead and noted the time of death for future reference. When the coroner was done wrapping the body, he saw that the blood was black on it instead of red. Draven informed the coroner that he noticed this as the killer was dying and blood was rushing out of its mouth due to numerous gunshots in the chest, which caused his lungs to fill up with blood. The coroner informed Draven that he would perform an autopsy and inform him of the results later in the week. They then proceeded to place the body in a gurney so it could be taken into a medical examination truck and transported to the coroner's office for autopsy.

Draven then went to the blood-draining lab where most of the task force was searching it for additional evidence. One of the detectives pulled out a scrapbook and talked about discovering it in a secret panel. The detective talked about thumbing through the scrapbook and finding numerous newspaper clippings documenting his kills and the police efforts to stop them. The detective informed Draven that the killer was especially fixated on his attempts to apprehend him and thought of it as a game of cat and mouse between them.

Draven looked through the scrapbook in a meticulous manner, and it confirmed that the killer selected his victims based on their blood type. The killer was using the Social Security Administration database to locate Social Security replacement card applications of young women who fit this criteria. They also found his fake documents, which included his California identification and Social Security cards and birth certificate. Draven gathered that the killer was planning to leave San Francisco and start over if he was in danger of being caught by law enforcement.

But one question still haunted Draven. The killer had a huge collection of newspaper clippings and other documents concerning the explosion and subsequent fire that took place in the Bayview/Hunter's Point neighborhood twenty years ago. Draven could not figure this out, but the answer to this riddle would soon emerge.

CHAPTER 131

A few days later, the coroner contacted Draven via telephone and wanted to talk to him about the results of the autopsy that he performed on the recently deceased serial killer. Draven scheduled an appointment to see the coroner later in the day in the medical examination office at nine and thanked him also for getting back to him pertaining to the results of the autopsy. The coroner reminded Draven that his office had been relocated to the basement of an office building several blocks away from the police station. The coroner then gave him the address of his office. The physical makeup of the killer sparked his curiosity since witnessing him bleed black instead of red blood after the fatal gunshot wound to his lungs. Draven had never witnessed this before, and now he would get answers as to why this happened.

Draven decided to finish up some paperwork before proceeding to the appointment with the coroner. He needed to fill out an incident report about the fatal shooting of the serial killer, which occurred a few days ago. In the incident report, Draven documented aspects surrounding the shooting, which included the suspect possessing a firearm and attempting to take his life with it. Additional information documented in the incident report pertained to the suspect oozing black blood instead of red after being shot fatally in the lungs. He also noted the demographics of the killer in the report. The killer was an older Caucasian male in his twenties, bald, and 5'8". He was slender and looked fairly normal for a serial killer, but Draven thought to himself, "They probably all look that way."

When done with the incident report, he presented it to Captain Hammer. Captain Hammer reviewed it and then filed the report away in a designated cabinet. This was done in case they were needed for any potential references in the future. Draven then informed the captain that he was going to see the coroner at his office to discuss the results of the autopsy done on the serial killer. Captain Hammer said, "Keep me posted."

Draven responded, "I will." He then left the police station to go to his appointment with the coroner in the medical examination room located a few blocks away.

CHAPTER 132

Draven proceeded to walk to the coroner's office for his appointment at nine. It was close to the police station, and Draven could use the exercise. He had been working in the office all day, completing the incident report and other paperwork. The walk would let him relax and allow his mind to wander. While walking to the coroner's office, he thought about the case. He had some lingering questions pertaining to it. Draven thought, *Why did the killer have newspaper clippings of the explosion and the subsequent fire that took place in the Bayview/Hunter's Point neighborhood twenty years ago in his scrapbook? It did not make sense, and hopefully, the meeting with the coroner would shed some light on this mystery.*

Draven arrived at his destination within minutes. The building was a tall, gray-monolith that rose high into the sky. He entered the building and went to the registry that listed office locations off to the side of the entranceway. Draven looked up the office number for the coroner's office and found that it was located in the basement of this building. He took the elevator to it and thought, "The location of this office is such a cliché." He also prayed that the cable in the elevator would not snap and plunge him onto the hard, cold surface down below. The elevator was creaky and wobbly, and Draven felt it was in dire need of a maintenance check.

CHAPTER 133

Draven arrived at the coroner's office. He knocked on the door, and the coroner let him in. Draven introduced himself to the coroner and informed him that he was there to review the results of the autopsy. Before proceeding any further, the coroner asked Draven, "Would you like to have a seat or something to drink?"

Draven declined the drink but said, "I would like a chair to sit on."

The coroner went to get a chair and presented it to Draven. Draven then sat down and proceeded to rest his tired, weary feet, ready to hear the results of the autopsy with intense, unrelenting curiosity.

While listening to the results of the autopsy, Draven looked at the layout and décor of the coroner's office. He noticed that the room was dark gray with little furniture, minus a desk in the left corner of it. Some bookshelves were present in the room, and they were filled with a vast assortment of books pertaining to human anatomy and crime scene investigation. On the coroner's desk, lay several pictures of a woman with a young child. Draven gathered that this was the coroner's wife and daughter. Hanging on the wall behind the coroner's desk were his college degrees from the University of San Francisco. Draven looked at them further and saw that one was a BA in psychology, while another was a MA in forensic science. On the right of the room stood the refrigeration unit, where the deceased bodies were stored after an autopsy and ready for burial. In front of the refrigeration unit stood the hard, cold, steel slabs, where autopsies were done, and Draven cringed when he thought about this.

Draven listened with intense, unwavering attention as the results of the autopsy were relayed to him. He heard the coroner inform him that this individual was a Caucasian male in his twenties, who died from suffocation due to blood filling up the lungs and impacting his ability to breathe. The coroner continued and went on to say that this was caused by several gunshot wounds to the chest, which penetrated the man's lungs. The coroner then talked about the vast amount of fentanyl and methamphetamine present throughout his body. He informed Draven that the enormous amount of these chemicals present in this body would have killed a normal human being and told him that the recently deceased had a blood type of AB-. The coroner talked about this being an extremely rare blood type and informed Draven that it was only present in 5 percent of the total population within the United States.

He went on to say that the recently deceased required a complete blood transfusion (all eight pints) every week; otherwise, he would die. He also informed Draven that the enormous amount of fentanyl and methamphetamine in his system slowly poisoned his body. The coroner told Draven that this accounted for the recently deceased looking older than his biological age and the black blood that oozed out of his body during the fatal gunshot wound that ripped through his lungs. The coroner then informed Draven that all the blood in the killer's body had turned black due to the huge amount of these two deadly chemicals present throughout his bloodstream.

After hearing the results of the autopsy, Draven was astonished and dumbfounded. Based on the chemical composition of the killer, it sounded and appeared as if this individual was not even human. He had a body, arms, legs, and all the internal organs of a human being, but the information left more unanswered questions. Draven almost became overwhelmed with his own internal thoughts until he heard the coroner begin to relay more information about the serial killer to him.

The coroner talked about having additional questions pertaining to the chemical composition and genetic structure of the serial killer. He shared Draven's concerns and thoughts about the killer having the biological and chemical structure of a human being but wondering if this individual was truly human. Based on these concerns, the coroner informed Draven that he sent the results to Dr. Hildebrand from UCSF for further examination and analysis. He was the leading figure in molecular biology and achieved groundbreaking results in the field. They both felt that he could make sense out of the results of the autopsy.

The coroner informed Draven that he received the results from Dr. Hildebrand yesterday and wanted to share them with him. Draven was on the edge of his seat and listened to every word of the coroner with unwavering attention. The coroner started by saying, "The killer's anatomy is almost composed entirely of fentanyl and methamphetamine, and this has poisoned his blood, accounting for its black color and the killer looking much older than his biological age. The killer needs to have all his blood changed once a week; otherwise he will die, and it needs to be AB-, which is an extremely rare blood type."

The coroner continued reading the report and emphasized that the next section proved interesting and was filled with brand-new information pertaining to the origin of the serial killer. "The killer had a large amount of additional chemicals present throughout his body. These are consistent with the chemicals used to create fentanyl and methamphetamine. In order for an amount this large to be present throughout the body, it required an incubation period, where the chemicals slowly coalesced and melded together. The incubation period was needed to provide a warm and humid environment. It would take twenty years for this process to complete itself, and the trigger point would be a loud, fiery explosion. The killer appears and looks human because dead bodies were absorbed in it. The skin and other body parts melded with the chemicals in the explosion to create the body that lies before you. This fits perfectly with an abandoned meth lab later converted to a blood-draining one by the killer."

Draven was completely floored by these developments and could feel his jaw dropping subconsciously on the ground. He said, "What you are saying is that he was born in that meth lab twenty years ago and the explosion and the subsequent fire created him? The same explosion and subsequent fire that took place in the Bayview/Hunter's Point neighborhood twenty years ago? Also, the killer's house was built over the meth lab that he later converted to a blood-draining one?"

The coroner said yes. The coroner had other information pertaining to the killer's origin to present to Draven. Draven did not know if he could take it anymore, but he continued to listen to every word that the coroner said. The coroner talked about attempting to obtain a birth certificate from the County Register's office via telephone from Phoenix, Arizona, for a Mr. William Harcourt. The killer had Phoenix, Arizona, listed as the city of birth. He spoke to a representative from the County Register's office who handled vital records such as birth certificates and was told it did not exist for someone matching this name. The killer had never been married or attempted to change his name, so that ruled out any possible name changes. The coroner talked about working with the County Register to locate other individuals with a similar name born on that date but obtained no matches. Therefore, the original birth certificate was fake, and that confirmed that Mr. Harcourt, the pure evil, was born in that meth lab twenty years ago.

Draven was shocked and speechless. He could not believe the information the coroner had presented to him pertaining to the origin of the killer. He assumed the killer was a human being targeting women because of some depraved, twisted, warped rationale that this monster could only comprehend. He never guessed that the killer was a creature camouflaged as a human being performing these acts of barbaric violence out of sheer survival. He wondered how many more of these sick monsters were out there roaming the streets, so he made it his mission to hunt them down. He would be the justice and retribution for their victims and would not rest until each one had been wiped away from this earth. That was his mission, and he embraced it with all his heart. He would be their avenging angel.

EPILOGUE

It was a great day at the beach. The sun was out, and it bounced, almost glistened, off the water. There was a slight breeze in the air, and everyone was completely relaxed. The seagulls were chirping and alerting everybody of their presence. The sun was bright and illuminated the entire beach. Little Jimmi was playing in the water and getting his fur soaked in the process. Asia was in a bathing suit, enjoying the fresh salty air with Draven, and all was right in the world. He had achieved paradise at last and could finally settle down to enjoy the fruits of all his work. He had finally reached his dream and obtained paradise on earth.

The End

ABOUT THE AUTHOR

Charles Porta was born and raised in San Francisco, California. He currently resides in Daly City, California, with his mother and two dogs, Little Jimmi and Rosie. He has a BA in psychology from San Francisco State University and a MA in counseling psychology from the University of San Francisco. He enjoys watching scary movies, attending rock-and-roll concerts, and spending time with his dogs. He is busy writing the follow-up to *Pure Evil*.